The aim of the *Earth Quest* series is to examine and explain how
shamanic principles can be applied in the journey towards self-discovery
– and beyond.

Each person's Earth quest is the search for meaning and purpose in their
life – it is the establishment of identity and the realization of inner
potentials and individual responsibility.

Each book in the series examines aspects of a life science that is in
harmony with the Earth and shows how each person can attune
themselves to nature. Each book imparts knowledge of the Craft of Life.

Earth Light

R. J. Stewart is a Scottish author and composer who has worked, researched and written extensively on the Western tradition. He has composed and recorded music for television, film and stage, and is the designer and player of the 80-stringed concert psaltery.

Earth Light

The Ancient Path to Transformation

*Rediscovering the Wisdom
of Celtic and Faery Lore*

R. J. Stewart

ELEMENT

Shaftesbury, Dorset ● Rockport, Massachusetts

Published in Great Britain in 1992 by
Element Books Limited
Longmead, Shaftesbury, Dorset

Published in the USA in 1992 by
Element, Inc
42 Broadway, Rockport, MA 01966

Cover illustration by Courtney Davis
Cover design by Max Fairbrother
Illustrations by Miranda Gray
Typeset by Poole Typesetting
Printed and bound in Great Britain by
Dotesios Ltd, Trowbridge, Wiltshire

British Library Cataloguing in Publication Data available

Library of Congress Cataloging in Publication Data available

ISBN 1–85230–243–7

How beautiful they are
The lordly ones
Who dwell in the hills,
In the hollow hills.

They have faces like flowers,
And their breath is a wind
That stirs amid grasses
Filled with white clover.

Their limbs are more white
Than shafts of moonshine:
They are more fleet
Than the March wind.

They laugh and are glad,
And are terrible:
When their lances shake and glitter
Every green reed quivers.

How beautiful they are,
How beautiful,
The lordly ones
In the hollow hills.

From *The Immortal Hour* by Fiona Macleod

This book is dedicated to the forgotten, unknown seers, seeresses, healers, singers, tellers, players of music and keepers of lore. They are our ancestors, and for them the Underworld and faery realm were ever present, ever living. They may be found there still today.

Note to the Reader

The techniques and exercises in this book can generate both temporary and permanent changes of consciousness within any individual or group. For balanced development you are advised to use them within the context of ideas and ethics outlined in the main text. As with all transformative techniques or traditions, responsibility for end results or effects rests solely with the user.

Contents

ACKNOWLEDGEMENTS

I would like to acknowledge the influence of the following people over a number of years in working with the faery tradition: Deirdre Green, Gareth Knight, Marko Galley. I must also acknowledge those who entered the Underworld and Faery Realm with me (and returned again) at many gatherings, workshops, seminars, ceremonies and visualizations between 1980 and 1991. Without their efforts and their willingness to discuss their experiences, much of this book could not have been written.

I should also acknowledge the inspiration and influence of the late Ewan MacColl, who introduced me to Scottish ballad singing when I was a teenager, and who was in every way the twentieth-century bard.

None of the people mentioned by name are responsible for my opinions and errors, and they may never have agreed with or supported the theories and practices in this book.

An earlier version of some of the material in Chapter 7 and the visualization *The Weaver Goddess* (page 106) was first published in my *Advanced Magical Arts*, Element Books, Shaftesbury, 1988.

Where is Paradise?

We are afraid to go into the Underworld, for there we must confront, if needs be, the shadows within ourselves. We long for the faery realm, yet if there is shadow left within our hearts, we will find its image there. Paradise is a step away and a step back, for in one image this planet, your land, all lands, are paradise, here, now. The imbalance arises from within us, and nowhere else. We have imaged and thought our way out of the primal world, drawing its shape with us, removing it from its perfect reality into a state that is uttered from our own awareness. Yet it is not enough now to simply declare 'let the world be perfect'. Just as we strove to materialize and degrade the world, shaping it according to our arrogance, so we must work to make it whole again. Paradise is not just the faery realm, nor the innocent past of the Earth; it is the living present in which the primal and perfect worlds are united. This unity comes through us; we are the bridge makers, the healers, the harmonizers. What we have collectively rejected and destroyed is the ever-present paradise, and we must learn how to seek it, find it, and realize it.

R. J. Stewart

Preface

Do you believe in faeries? Our ancestors certainly did, from as recently as the twentieth century to the remote past, and not the Disney variety with pretty gossamer wings and coy expressions. If you thought that faeries were little people, please think again. They were, and are, usually said to be of human size or taller. What if faeries are real beings and what if there are powerful ancient traditions of deep change, of inner transformation, connected to them and to their realm? Nothing like modern faery tales or Victorian sentiment, nothing like Tinkerbell in Peter Pan. Such fantasies are not and never have been part of the living faery tradition.

In the following chapters I invite you to examine genuine faery-lore, presented as a modern summary and fresh statement of an ancient transformative tradition. This is not a book on folklore or anthropology, but on the power of the imagination to open our perceptions and radically alter our relationship to nature.

I also invite you to work with some meditative and visualizing exercises that establish contact with the faery realm and its inhabitants. No space is wasted on a complex intellectual argument or on statistical or other 'proofs', though there are many that might be put forward. Nor is there any sentiment, vague moralizing or escapist romanticism, such as are frequently found in the worst fiction on faery themes written in the last 200 years.

The faery beings are potentially powerful allies, yet if you enter their realm for the wrong reasons, may become terrible opponents. This interesting question of polarity, defined according to your true intent, is discussed in later chapters. Everything in the faery realm is intensified, amplified, sometimes painfully or ecstatically real. I should state at this point that it is not a hallucinatory or drug-related vision, and that the changes of consciousness are all brought about by natural means. Such means are well within our own unaided, undrugged, inherent abilities to vary our perceptions and energies.

You may explore the faery realm for yourself if you follow the methods laid out in this book. It is not a fantasy land, not a childish escape, but the primal land *within*; both within our consciousness and within the planet. It is not simply something that we imagine, for it has a true nature and firm identity of its own, existing even if you never think of it. The inhabitants of the faery realm are beautiful and terrible, inspiring and disturbing. If you go there, you will emerge changed. Do not take my word for this but try the methods described. Experience and judge for yourself.

I have worked with this material for over fifteen years and so have many other people, working with me in groups or using the methods and recorded visualization from my earlier book *The Underworld Initiation*. Such work is in harmony with that of many others through the centuries, both known and unknown, seers, poets, musicians, artists, and thousands of ordinary people. Out of all the so-called esoteric traditions, the faery initiations have always been in the special care of ordinary men and women, particularly those who lived and worked close to the land.

Exploring the faery realm is one aspect of an even more obscure and potent perennial wisdom tradition, that of the Underworld. At the very foundations of religion, mysticism and magic is an almost forgotten concept of power and light, not revealed in the sky or far away in divine dimensions but utterly close, below and within the Earth. Regeneration of all life, according to the ancients, came from beneath the land, from a realm ruled by a dark goddess of death and rebirth. Her pervasive cycles of life energy and change apply to all beings.

The sacredness of the land and planet is a major concern for us today, and the attraction of ancestral techniques and world-views should not be as childish means of escape from responsibility. The perennial world-views or wisdom traditions hold within themselves potentially balancing and materially responsible experiences. If we are concerned about the land, the planet, the environment, we will have to change ourselves; we are the land, the environment ... we are not separate from one another.

We will have to change ourselves before we can bring about a new image and reality that will restore the holism of land and living beings and heal the effects of the destruction that we have wrought. The power for this change rests not exclusively in the human imagination but in the Underworld, the realm of potentials, of regenerative forces that are, for us, activated through various imaginative and physical means.

The true faery teachings are part of this Underwold lore, powerful traditions in which humanity, the land and the planet interact with one another, often through the agency of non-material or non-organic beings. Foremost among them is the faery race. If you feel, as I do, that humanity has wilfully separated itself from the idea of the sacred land and the regenerative Mother Earth, then you may find the faery and Underworld traditions to be a powerful path towards reunion. If you take this path you will find the way to the faery realm, and to other realms within the Underworld. Upon these unusual less-travelled ways, you will discover and eventually begin to mediate the Light within the Earth.

This book contains information on basic techniques for entering the Underworld, concentrating for the major part upon the faery realm, which is that zone of the Underworld closest to our own lands. I have also included some short personal accounts of my own Underworld and faery experiences, and reported various effects and typical encounters from group work over a period of years with varying groups in different places.

The first part of the book is a short summary of the Underworld and faery realms, putting the old traditions into a contemporary context. The second part consists of exercises, techniques and some general guiding material to support individual and group work. There is an emphasis upon doing-it-yourself and moving the tradition onwards into our collective future.

Earth Light is dedicated to all walkers between the worlds, whoever, whenever, whatever, they may be.

R. J. Stewart

Introduction

As this is a book for our intuition, imagination and inspiration, I do not feel that it is necessary to discuss or 'prove' the existence of the Underworld and its realms, including the faery realm. They are affirmed by ancient traditions worldwide, and it is up to us in the modern age to make our own decisions based upon intuition, experience and common sense. The reality of one age becomes the delusion of another, as materialist science has amply proven, not least of itself.

The first significant question is not one of proof or disproof, but why might we seek to encounter and explore the faery realm? Rather than debate intellectually over its existence and nature, why bother approaching it at all? The answers may be found in tradition, but are also directly relevant to our contemporary situation.

Part of the potential value of Underworld and faery realm traditions is that they are inherent in our collective consciousness; everyone has always said that they are there. This universal recognition and acceptance should not be underestimated or confused with mere ignorance and superstition. There are complex power traditions associated with the faery realm, varying from land to land, people to people. Because of their endurance, these ubiquitous traditions may be worth reassessing and activating in a modern context. In this book we will be focusing upon the broad stream of Underworld and faery traditions of the so-called Western world, which includes Europe, Russia and, through relationship, America, Canada, Australia and New Zealand. The last four regions of the planet have distinct, profound native traditions of their own, sharing much in common with the Underworld and faery traditions of Europe but not with the political and dogmatic spiritual traditions of Europe or with intellectual occultism. We will not, however, be making any comparisons of folklore or customs in an academic sense, as there are many excellent reference books that already do this; a short list of these sources is given in the References and Bibliography.

The faery races, according to tradition, are different in each different land, and I do not claim to present even a fraction of the ethnic and tribal lore concerning faery beings known worldwide. The principles of the Underworld techniques, however, will work wherever you may be.

The fundamental lore, which means the collective or traditional imagery, used in the visualizations and reported evidence of this book derives primarily from that of European people through the ages, with some emphasis upon Celtic tradition, as this is one of the classic primal traditions concerning the faery realm.

Like all primal or esoteric traditions, the faery tradition is not obligatory. It is merely one way, one path, one set of encounters. It does not carry any dogma, religious weight or ethical obligation. This may make it more dangerous for the individual than, say, the spiritual path of a world religion. But it is free of the corruption of politics and soul enslavement that we find in many orthodox religions. The interplay between orthodox religion and the primal traditions is curious, and much misrepresented today by both pro- and anti-pagans. In past centuries in Europe, many seers, poets, musicians, or healers, working directly with faery beings as allies, were also churchgoers. This simple historical fact is often passed over in our modern revival of paganism, and it is not merely a matter of politics or social obligation.

Upon the deepest levels, primal Christianity, which appeared in the West through travelling evangelists out of Roman-Greek and Middle-Eastern cultures, merged successfully with the pagan religions. Conflict only appeared at a much later stage, when the political and material gains of the late Roman Empire, suddenly becoming officially Christian, were at stake.[1] There is an interaction between the Underworld traditions, in actual practice rather than in theory or esoteric philosophy, and the power of untainted Christianity. We shall be examining this interaction in *Power within the Land*, a companion volume to this book which deals with the deepest realms and traditions of the Underworld.

Setting this theme of the relationship between pagan and Christian aside for the moment, let us consider possible reasons for encountering and exploring the faery realm and meeting its inhabitants. We need not think of such reasons exclusively as continuations of any esoteric tradition (even though this is the case) but in terms of intrinsic potential and value today. If we find no value in something, whatever it may be, there is no obligation to undertake it.

By value, however, we need not mean material benefit or selfish gain; there are many relative qualities and potential events and encounters of value in the great adventure of spiritual and inner development. It is the greatest of all adventures, within which all others are encompassed. Our outer world is progressively diminished and corrupted by abuse of technology, greed and indifference to the welfare of other orders of life, and romantic adventurers often complain that there is nothing left to explore, no liberating challenge or experience. But liberation comes from within, both within ourselves and within the Underworld that is the original source and image for our planet.

THE PRIMAL LAND AND THE POLLUTED PLANET

Before we begin to discuss the inhabitants of the faery realm, those people of the Sidhe known in Celtic tradition and in related folk traditions worldwide under many names, we should briefly consider the faery realm itself. If we reduced the vast mass of descriptions and beliefs down to basics, what would they be? The faery realm has a consistent appearance in accounts that have been handed down to us both from seers and from ordinary people, from sources in myth, legend and humble folk-tales. Clearly it involves some inherited images from formal religious pagan traditions of the Underworld/Otherworld, but it also has a coherent and persistent individuality, which continues right through into twentieth-century accounts.

The faery realm is the Primal Land: wherever you are, whatever land you are in, the faery realm is the primal image of that land. It is before and beyond corruption and pollution, hence its legendary names: the Ever Young, the Land of Heart's Desire. This does not mean that the faery realm or realms (for there are more than one) are stereotypically idyllic, innocent or static; they have their cycles of energy and their terrors. For us, the first, and perhaps today the most important, aspect is that the faery realm *mirrors* our own.

After some exploration and experience, the techniques of which come in later chapters, we might feel that our world is devolved or reflected *out of* the primal image of the faery world. It is in this sense of devolution or fall that early Christianity and the faery traditions concerning the separation of the realms originally met and agreed with one another. The essential difference is that there is no dogma of sin or damnation in the older traditions, such as were subsequently introduced into Christianity for purpose of suppression and control.

In mystical definitions, and in spiritual traditions handed down to us, the faery realm is consubstantial with the Lunar World or general environment of the Earth and Moon. In Gaelic (Celtic) tradition, and in the perennial Underworld tradition, it is found, literally, *within the body of the planet.*

More specifically, it is an Underworld mirror image of the land in which you live . . . but a pristine image, out of which your own land is extended, reflected, distorted or even devolved. We all carry such an image within us, it is a shared dream of humanity. Rather than it being an ideal or a product of dogma, the ancient traditions assert that this image that we have deep within us is our memory of, and intuition about, the primal land inherent within our manifest land. This land is in the Underworld, not heaven or paradise, and one of its major zones is the faery realm.

Seemingly the two images, the primal land and the manifest land, were once close together; humans and the faery people once mingled freely, even intermarried. So we are told in a vast range of myths, legends, folk tales, narrative ballads and initiatory themes from around the world. In time the two realms separated. Many reasons are suggested for this separation, ranging from the most obscure esoteric propositions and intellectual teachings to religious propaganda, to pseudo-evolutionary mysticism. Everyone tries to rationalize loss.

A very direct proposition, my own for this book, might be that our inherent isolationism, greed, aggression, and rejection of all living beings and of the land itself, has led to our separation. We have no one to blame but ourselves . . . not temptation, not evolution or devolution, not the faery beings. We are responsible for whatever we have done. We shall return to this hard theme again.

The connection and subsequent separation between the faery and human realms and their peoples is not a matter of time-lost legend or ancient myth, for as recently as the seventeenth century the Reverend Robert Kirk outlined in detail the faery practices of the Gaelic seers of Scotland.[2] Only 300 years ago it was commonplace for people to see faery beings of different types, to converse with them, to pass *physically* in and out of the Underworld or faery realms. So the Reverend Kirk and others report. Such reports persisted from Scotland, Ireland, Wales, Brittany and parts of south-west England into the twentieth century, and remain within living memory today.[3]

Three distinct classes of encounter are frequently reported: those with faery beings, those with the ancestral spirits of humans, and those with humans physically transported to the faery realm. Tradition makes clear distinctions between these three, and they form the basis of a very ancient and powerful initiatory system for transforming consciousness and energy.

I have called this the *Underworld Initiation,* a term that I originated in articles and group work in the 1970s and later used as the title for my first book on this tradition. The manuscript was written in 1978 and circulated privately for several years before publication[4]. The Underworld Initiation is quite distinct from modern ideas such as spiritualism, New Age channelling, psychism and so forth, which seek to rationalize certain imaginative or inner events into meaningful systems isolated from the body of ancient tradition and collective lore. We shall return to these differences again as we progress. Usually the isolation is due to simple ignorance, but separation from our primal traditions is also a result of religious educational and commercial conditioning, and has many negative implications that still resonate through New Age spirituality.[5]

The 'second sight' of the Gaelic people, integral to faery lore, was the subject of much debate and some research in the seventeenth, eighteenth and nineteenth centuries. Dr Johnson, the famous English man of letters, reported that a temporary gift of the sight could be obtained in exchange for a bag of tea (a great delicacy in his day); the Reverend Kirk describes two initiatory methods by which the second sight is conferred either temporarily or permanently.[6]

Second sight, though famous in a Celtic context, is known in many other races and lands worldwide. It is not necessarily identifiable with spiritualism and clairvoyance, though modern writers have often attempted to make such identifications. Second sight is part of a specific tradition with firm techniques, well-described beings, visions, and a long history of oral teaching. The content and effect are different from that of modern psychic experiments or popular clairvoyance. The reasons for this are various, and we shall discuss some of them in later chapters.

The second sight of Celtic and northern European tradition often runs in families, as does the faery healing touch: both were active up to the early years of the twentieth century, and were widely reported in Britain in Devon, Cornwall, Wales, Scotland and Ireland. Both second sight and healing techniques frequently involved the use of allies or faery companions and co-walkers. The term co-walker was coined by Robert Kirk in his report of faery traditions, translated from the Gaelic seers' special term for faery beings that specifically aid such seers. Other terms such as messengers, allies, companions and doubles are found in various contexts from the classical writings of the ancient world to the present day.

These beings should not be confused with the 'astral double' or 'astral body' in modern occult literature, which is used to mean the phantom or temporary dream-body, the opposite of the original meaning of the term astral body which was a body or spiritual state in the realm of the stars. Similarly the 'astral plane' of popular and Victorian occultism is not the faery realm or Underworld but the phantom world of thought forms, emotional shells and other discarnate entities with no true soul or spiritual awareness: they are replays with limited repetitious functions. These are the trivial echoes that appear in spiritualist seances, and nowadays cause 'channelling'.

Faery healing often took place at a distance, with some unusual and distinctive techniques reported by seventeenth-century and later writers. These included removing bullets and other objects from a wounded man at a distance, and the seer or healer reportedly spitting the object out into a bowl of water, as if it had been transported mysteriously out of the wound into his or her mouth. I do not make any claims for such reports as I have had no experience of distant healing using faery allies, but the technique was very widespread in Celtic regions up to the seventeenth and eighteenth centuries, and in the early years of the twentieth century folklorists were still collecting tales of such healing arts.

The seventeenth-century military mind was much preoccupied with such marvels as protection against bullets, distant healing and the suspect ability of being able to see events and persons at a distance. Samuel Pepys (notorious for his sexually candid diaries and famous as the effective civil founder of the modern British Navy) was sent to Spain to investigate seers there. Although these traditional seers and magicians were renowned for their far vision, Pepys' report was inconclusive.[7]

In Kirk's day, the late seventeenth century, various military officers and scientists were concerned about the Scots' abilities to protect themselves against wounds or to spy out invading English armies (this was shortly after the English Revolution and Commonwealth). The same concern is still shown today by the Pentagon and its Russian counterparts, though telepathy is given a vaguely scientific respectability.

The proper place for the encounters of the faery realm is, initially, in the attuned imagination, and for beneficial transformative purposes with no ulterior or selfish motives. Whatever motives we may have are reflected back to us in the faery realm, hence the traditional requirement that we be pure of heart, steadfast of will and honest. Deceit breeds deceit, and greed acquires only faery gold, which turns to leaves in daylight. What we should seek, perhaps, are the leaves of the trees in the faery realm, which turn to regenerative gold in our upper world, the gold of a restored healthy environment.

There is no claim in this book that such marvels as distant faery or allied healing may be done today, or even that in the past they were all free of style, sham or sleight of hand. I leave this to further experiment, exploration and experience. What is important is that techniques were widely known in which second sight and healing were connected to the alliance of faery beings. We shall return to this subject again, but for the present we are assessing the basic traditions of the faery realm as an Otherworld land attuned to our own, wherever it may be.

ENVIRONMENT AND TRANSFORMATION

The primal land within the earth is, seemingly, far from us today. To restore our own land, our planet, to a state of balance is a major task for humanity. And so it must be, for we are individually and collectively responsible for the poisoning of our lands, our seas, our world.

One method of restoring the land to health is through working with the image of the primal land within the polluted land. This involves bringing the outer and inner, upper- and under-worlds together; we should seek to unite the human realm with the faery realm. If this is a valid and workable technique, and if we are able to reattune our land to the faery land, we may gain regeneration and rebalance. Whatever we may imagine, make empowered images of, comes to outer manifestation.

Ideally the two realms, Over- and Underworld, should balance one another; whatever is found in one has a reflection or polar partner or opposite in the other. This includes humans and other, non-human, beings, a subject to which we shall return in later chapters. A simple illustration of this perennial tradition is found in Figure 1.

There is a collection of special techniques for enhancing our energies, and which enable our interaction with the faery realm. These are embedded within the initiatory tradition of the Underworld, a tradition which reaches back to prehistory. Until recently such traditions were preserved either in a diffuse form in folklore or among a few people who had received the teachings orally. This special oral teaching, widespread within the context of myth and legend in earlier centuries, is virtually extinct today. Both the deeper Underworld techniques and the traditions concerning the faery realm, however, may be brought back for modern use. If these teachings and the dynamic techniques that they contain are effective, they hold a key to a means of regeneration, both individually and environmentally.

We should be aware that, in the past, the Underworld and faery traditions, as initiatory arts rather than as diffuse folklore, were traditions of *inner power*. The impetus for uniting the realms and

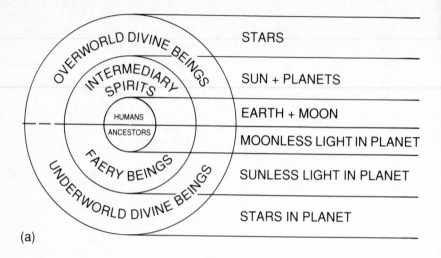

STARS

SUN + PLANETS

EARTH + MOON

MOONLESS LIGHT IN PLANET

SUNLESS LIGHT IN PLANET

STARS IN PLANET

(a)

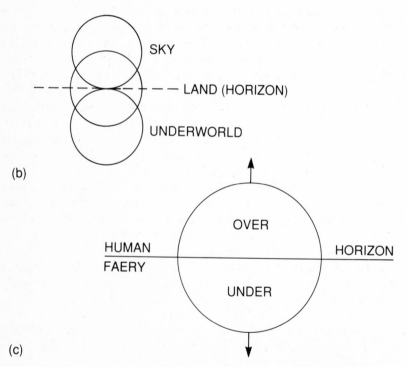

SKY

LAND (HORIZON)

UNDERWORLD

(b)

(c)

Figure 1(a) Overworld and Underworld Inhabitants
Figure 1(b) The Three Worlds or Environments
Figure 1(c) The Mirroring of Human and Faery Realms

regenerating the outer world may not have been present in distant centuries, as the worlds were much closer together. While ordinary people had regular communication and encounters with faery beings, seers and initiates worked with the deeper levels of such encounters, using the energy of the Underworld for empowerment.

Any number of motives, of course, can lead to the quest for power, ranging from sacrificial selflessness to ultimate delusion and greed.

In this book we shall explore and experience techniques that have a twofold effect. Firstly they transform us. Secondly they give us the means to regenerate our land, our world. I feel that the individual should balance his or herself between these two aims. We cannot seek to regenerate the land unless we have the power to do so. There are, in one sense, three aspects of this Underworld initiatory teaching. The first is the power tradition, which can be confined solely to individual development with no spiritual or selfless motive. The second is its polar opposite, the sacrificial tradition, in which the individual is willing to give up all for the land, the people. We shall examine this major theme in *Power within the Land*.

The third is what I would call the environmental tradition, and this can be restated for today. It involves reducing our separation from, and antagonism towards, the planet through a series of cathartic meditative or visualizing experiences. Techniques for this are found in our later chapters, mainly in Part Two. Once our barriers are lowered, the energy locked up within them is available for inner transformation. And more, for we can tap into our Underworld energies, long neglected, ignored or denied, through specific techniques such as the exercises in Chapters 4 to 7.

In the environmental tradition, the faery realm and beings are of great importance. They are deeply interwoven with the forces of nature in the over- and under-worlds. Many insights into our natural world and its subtle energies are conferred through interaction with the faery realm. This is an ancient teaching, and my own role has been to explore and redefine it for today. I did not invent it, though the techniques offered in this book are my own specific and original versions written for individual and group work.

THE SEDUCTIVE LONGING FOR FAERYLAND

The faery realm is seductive. Indeed, it is the most seductive Otherworld, for it seeks always to fulfil our essential longing for the perfect land, the primal planet. This longing is strong, stronger than the wish-fulfilment paradisaical longings of orthodox (often patriarchal and therefore male-orientated) religion, for it stirs something essential deep within our souls, our bodies, our bones, our ancestral core of memories. The call of the faery realm is heard and felt by men and women and, of course, by children who may be nearer to it in their souls than adults.

Many people find that entering the faery world is painful, for the recognition and joy and purity of that realm come vibrantly alive from seeds buried within our souls. Leaving that place becomes a burden; returning to the grey, dull, wilfully poisoned, abused and polluted human world becomes a penance, a terrible sentence of imprisonment. How may we respond to this seduction . . . if seduction is the right word for our inherent and proper primal longing for a perfect land, for regenerative darkness and the transformative light within the earth?

Seduction is, ultimately, an individual matter; that which seduces or even corrupts one person is merely attractive for another, undesirable and trivial to a third. The seduction of the faery realm, irresistible as it may seem at times, is intimately about our own awareness, particularly that of our emotions and sexuality. If we are willing to be drawn unconditionally into the faery realm and want to remain there solely to escape from our own world, then the seductive weakness *within ourselves* is a cause of delusion.

If, on the other hand, we enter the Underworld and the faery realm to bring back with us the primal image, the power of a purified and light-filled land, to transform ourselves and our corrupted world, then we have won through a major part of the test.

Let us not be in doubt for one moment; the faery realm is full of tests, challenges and tasks, any of which may turn to good or ill, according to our choice. The wish to bring the faery power back into the world is not merely an intellectual affirmation; it has to come from your heart, from understanding, out of compassion for all that suffer upon and within our planet.

Yes, you can enter the faery realm and remain there; according to tradition many have done so. But what are your reasons for being there? Are they selfish, or do they have a degree of selflessness, of sharing, of giving to regenerate the sacred land? The choice is yours, and most seductive of all, perhaps, is the simple fact that there is no blame, reaction, indictment or cause-and-effect in response to your decision. The laws of the faery realm, in the sense of cycles of apparent cause-and-effect or natural laws, are different from our own; they are discussed in the following chapters. The implications of this time difference are important in many aspects of the tradition.

In Western religious orthodoxy, the faery realm and its mirror of nature within our own world were bitterly opposed as a source of 'temptation'. People were ordered to defy nature, to resist this temptation, and to banish sternly all longings for the faery realm, all communication with its inhabitants, faery or ancestral. If necessary, believers were encouraged to seek the help of priests who would confirm the 'evil' of such contacts and longings, even ritually banishing them by force.

Orthodox religion taught that nature was a snare and a delusion, while faeryland was either hell or paid service to hell. Yet for centuries the common people in every land preserved an undercurrent of faery lore, faery-related traditions and ceremonies which state religion found it impossible to uproot. Materialism and television entertainment, however, have now almost finished the destructive task begun so long ago by the Church . . . why bother with faeryland when we can have soap operas? The sacred land is irrelevant in a pop-video consumer culture.

So the worlds move further apart, and our planet suffers just as our souls suffer from such manipulation, abuse and unnatural practices originally begun in the name of 'God'. The ultimate conclusion of this hostile or indifferent attitude to nature and the hidden worlds within nature is the unleashing of nuclear fission. Science has manifested the greatest self-destructive arrogance of materialism, derived directly from the nature-hating, planet-abusing political religions. What does it matter if we destroy the very fabric of the planet, when the elect will be praising God in heaven, and well out of it all?

We might note that there is no return from heaven . . . it is a one-way ticket. The primal land, the Underworld, the faery realm are all, in effect, exchangeable with our own; we may enter, return, and travel back and forward at will. This cycle of movement is often misinterpreted as reincarnation, but while the Celtic seers acknowledged a cycle of lives, they made several distinctions between this and passing in and out of the faery realm. The most obvious is the repeated tradition of people translated *physically* to the Underworld or faeryland and returning bodily, or sometimes remaining there as physical humans, out of the time cycle of the human world. There can be no confusion between clearly stated traditions of this sort and perennial philosophies concerning reincarnation or the journey of the soul, though these also have a firm role in the primal traditions worldwide.

The nearest comparison in popular modern literature is in the techniques described at length by Carlos Castaneda in his books upon a native American tradition of sorcery. A key event in this system (despite its much disputed sources) is physical translation into other dimensions, and subsequent physical return. Castaneda also describes a tradition in which adepts move physically into the other worlds and take a core group of magicians with them, but connected to an outer group still working in the human world. Such techniques existed centuries before Castaneda began to publish his books, and were well known in European magical and shamanistic traditions, both in direct teachings and through academic surveys of folklore and anthropology.

This walking between worlds is one of the so-called 'secret' teachings of the Northern and Western traditions, and we can presume that all variants come from collective wisdom or folklore concerning the relationship between worlds, and the traditions of physical movement between realities. The Celts preserved and taught it among seers and seeresses from the earliest times to as late as the twentieth century. In isolated country regions among ordinary people, accidental and intentional stepping between worlds was widely known and experienced, as ample evidence from researchers and scholars shows. It also formed part of the unpublicized teachings of esoteric or magical orders from classical times to the present day; I was taught something similar in the 1960s, though in a different context from that of the Underworld or faery tradition. So the idea is by no means unique to native American tradition and certainly did not originate in publication with Castaneda, even though his controversial teachings have had value in bringing it a wider modern public.

The ancestral contacts of the Underworld, many of which are awakened through entering the faery realm (but not exclusively confined to this) are quite distinct from physical humans in faeryland. They are distinct again, but less obviously so in some cases, from the faery beings themselves. While this traditional stream of lore may seem superficially confusing, it depends upon a holism of the worlds. Perennial wisdom teachings, of which the Underworld traditions are an essential aspect, were holistic rather than separatist.

If we allow ourselves to be trapped into a divisive or antagonistic mode of labelling, then we have to unpick strands of faery lore that are, in truth, closely intertwined. Separate them and we lose the reality altogether. One of the best visions of the holism of the worlds is found in Plato's *Republic* (the *Myth of Er*), and this classical world-view was upheld, in its Celtic form, well into modern times by Gaelic seers and seeresses.

We find it described in the seventeenth century by the Reverend Robert Kirk, in his *Secret Commonwealth*, and well attested in the large twentieth-century collection of faery traditions by W. Y. Evans Wentz.

Before going further into the faery realm and discussing its people, places and powers, I would like to place this widespread tradition, and the deeper embracing tradition of the Underworld, in a more immediate modern context. In the next chapter I will briefly discuss the Underworld Initiation, a set of transformative experiences leading to knowledge of Earth Light. This includes some examples of my own encounters with this tradition, and the associated traditions of the faery realm and its occupants. In the second part of the book, there are exercises for direct experience of the Underworld in visualization, and for energetic contact with Underworld forces that flow between the land and humanity.

The Underworld material holds the keys to many confused and restricted areas of magic, wisdom teachings, myth, legend and mysticism. We cannot fully work within the faery realm without the power and wisdom of the embracing Underworld tradition.

Part 1

1. Earth Light

REGENERATION

In the late 1970s I realized that working with the Underworld and faery traditions could be a major way of inner transformation. The traditions were well described, preserved in folklore and myth, religion and genuine magical arts (as distinct from popular 'occultism'), but had been passed over or ignored in the modern revival of interest in personal, transpersonal or spiritual transformation. Our tragic separation from the sacred land, inherent within the Underworld tradition, has made us strangers to a powerful truth.

The New Age movement, if such a term may be used, places great emphasis on rising towards light above and leaving things of Earth and darkness behind. This type of light-escapism is not found in working with the Underworld or faery realm, yet the world below, passing through and beyond darkness, is filled with light. The Underworld tradition affirms that universal wisdom and regeneration are not found exclusively in heavenly or ethereal dimensions, but also in the heart of the sacred land, the planet, within Mother Earth.

It also affirms that we are all, individually and collectively, responsible for the planet, and that in transforming ourselves we transform the world. To do this we can seek transformation within the Underworld, drawing upon the foundations of energies that uphold and regenerate the primal planet.

The primal planet is the perfect image, the realized potential of our Mother Earth. What restricts and imbalances that potential is ourselves, you, me, everyone. We are all responsible for the shadow cast over the world, and by bringing out the Earth Light, we can work towards regeneration. That light is found by passing within and below, light born out of darkness rather than light 'opposed to' darkness. As long as we think in terms of opposites and conflicting dualities we will feed aggression, wanton destruction, isolation.

The Underworld traditions teach that light and darkness are both emitted from a single source, within the land, within the planet. The ancient rhythm of the seasons shows a planetary cycle that passes from darkness to light and back to regenerative darkness again. This is due to the movement of the planet around the Sun; natural energies within the land are stimulated by such movement. The same patterns and tides of energy are reflected within ourselves ... our bodies are regenerated every moment out of the living substance of the land, the food and water that we take into ourselves. There is no antagonism between spirit and matter in the human being, only in the deluded human mind that isolates itself from the holism of the land and planet.

All ancient wisdom traditions teach that humanity and the land are one: destroy and pollute the land and we destroy and pollute ourselves. The Underworld traditions, ruthlessly opposed, distorted through propaganda, and suppressed for centuries, hold the key to our regeneration. The exploration and realization of various realms in the Underworld can no longer be confined to a few seers, magicians or initiates into ancient orders. The restoration of the planet is our collective and individual responsibility, here, now.

At its deepest levels, the Underworld tradition leads us to a realization of universal consciousness within; not merely within our minds but within the planet. This is a great mystical truth made manifest: the stars are within the Earth.

The world of our planet is the universal world. There is no vast spatial 'out there', no terrifying emptiness to theorise over, no Star Trek final frontier requiring high-tech transport. The reality is within the planet. Working directly with this realization in meditation eventually makes profound changes to our consciousness and energy, but such transformations begin with a simple suspension of our contemporary intellectual world-view.

This world-view is, after all, merely the product of recent Christian materialist conditioning. In its present form it has only existed for about a century and a half, beginning with the nineteenth-century scientific revolution that challenged Christian dogma concerning the Creation. The challenge extended, of course, to the dogma of all religions as Western science extended around the planet.

Beneath the illusory liberation of the materialist approach are centuries of Christian religious orthodox conditioning which, ironically, led to the hard materialist world-view that is so inimical to spiritual understanding. We do not have to subscribe to it, nor is it likely to endure for much longer in the upsurge of so-called new physics. This new school of physics is restating (to its own satisfaction) universal truths long known and taught worldwide in our perennial spiritual traditions.

The Underworld tradition, which exists in all cultures worldwide, affirms that if you go underground you find light; the light transforms and regenerates. Although science tells us that the material core of the planet is molten, this physical truth is but one possible state, expression or condition associated with the body of our world. Our own bodies are made up mainly of water, yet when we pass within in imagination and meditation we do not find our awareness soggily dissolving into cellular fluid. The body of the planet and, more locally, of the land in which we live, have their inner dimensions of energy and consciousness, just as the human body does. Our entities, humans and planet alike, are not solely confined to their physical manifestation.

If we descend into the land, into the planet, we find that there are realms within, and that these realms are populated. This theme is found in all oral traditions, preserved as folk tales, ancestral teachings, songs and ballads.

The descent takes various forms; it can be a very simple technique of visualizing yourself passing into the ground and through it into another dimension. The imagery is defined by a tradition, usually a collective or ancestral tradition, such as that of the faery realm which we will explore in later chapters. The experience is powerful and often surprising. I have worked with many people who felt that they would only encounter darkness, coldness, damp, worms, and so forth, yet when they passed through into the light below were both astonished and delighted. They were also transformed.

The descent into the Underworld has an effect not only upon our imagination or visualizing consciousness, but upon our entire organism and energy patterns. Again we find that it is not negative or devolving, but that it links us to areas of our being that we had lost, forgotten or excluded.

The linking and reawakening includes changes upon very deep levels, particularly that of the blood. This aspect of the tradition was a so-called 'secret' of spiritual and magical arts, and much nonsense is talked and written by people who have had no real experience of it. In practice we need not concern ourselves with this organic transformation too closely . . . it happens without analysis, explanation or pseudo-scientific rationalization. By passing within, into the Underworld, we extend our consciousness into the body of the land and simultaneously into our own bodies. Changes occur when we do this.

SOME EXPERIENCES IN THE UNDERWORLD AND FAERY REALM

The Underworld Initiation

From 1977 onwards, but particularly in 1978–80, I had a series of Underworld experiences which were, at that time, quite outside anything known to me. I had been practising meditation and visualization within the North-Western tradition since about 1968, working with Sacred Space, the Four Elements and specific innerworld or spiritual themes and contacts. None of these had any obvious Underworld sources or relationships that I understood or that I had been instructed in, though in retrospect there were many valuable connections to be made.

There is a curious situation within the arts of changing consciousness: they gradually and inevitably alter our understanding of both ourselves and of the arts themselves. First there is a mountain, then there is no mountain, then there is a mountain. This interaction is not a product of conditioning, familiarity or regular experience and maturity, for it underpins yet also transcends these time-based and habit-grown overlays of consciousness.

I eventually realized that without the Underworld Initiation most techniques of transformation, such as meditation and visualization, are either ineffective or top-heavy. Ineffective because they do not draw upon our most fundamental energies, and top-heavy because they rely solely upon rising into higher consciousness without resolving or acknowledging our relationship to the sacred land and planet. There is a stereotypical, spiritual, magical, 'New Age' type of person who is all energetic in the head and, more blessedly, in the heart, but all unaware or disdainful of anything below. Once such people were concerned with 'purity' and 'spirituality': today it is more likely to be 'chakras' and release from 'karma'.

We reject the fundamental energies of the Underworld at our greatest peril ... this rejection manifests as our appalling lack of relationship to our mother planet, to the land. It also manifests in our bodies as increasingly incurable syndromes: by polluting the land, the planet, we poison ourselves beyond cure or redemption. There is no cause and effect in this situation ... corruption of the planet and collective self-poisoning are the same act, beginning and ending with a wilful separation from the Light within the Earth, the sacredness of living matter. Now, having intellectually realized our potential fate, we have the arrogance to declare that a New Age will cure it all, and that if we shed negativity and guilt we can float off into realms of spiritual bliss!

As a result of my Underworld experiences in the late 1970s and early 1980s, I felt that the traditions of spiritual and transpersonal development, as they were represented in the current revival (of which I was a member), were woefully incomplete. They lacked that essential journey into the depths (not a psychic or emotional trauma) undertaken by all ancient seers, seeresses, priests, priestesses and seekers after truth. In the classical Mysteries, such as those of Isis made famous to us through the *Golden Ass* of Apuleius, this light within the Earth, found through journeying in darkness, was known as *The Sun at Midnight*. In time I was to publish some of my first reactions as *The Underworld Initiation*, a book that dealt directly with the techniques and realizations inherent within certain traditions of the Underworld that had been ignored or deliberately passed over in the modern revival of esoteric arts. It seemed essential, then, to show that original Northern and Western traditions contained a method of psychic transformation that was unknown to either the old school occultists and Theosophists or the burgeoning New Age collection of movements and beliefs.

My own first experience came, without seeking, in a series of dreams. These were disturbing and difficult but had a profound effect upon me, causing me to bring the entire experience out into conscious meditation and visualization. Having done so, I found that it could be communicated successfully to others, as if the initial pioneering experience had borne some of the weight, taking it away from those who would follow. There are now several thousand people worldwide who have the guided visualization tape *Journey to the Underworld*, and the experience has been developed in groups for the last ten years or so with increasing success. Despite this alleviation, because anything seeded into the collective consciousness is easier for those that follow the initial birth-pains of the experience, the Underworld Initiation is not any easy path.

The dreams that arose for me were demanding and repeated themselves in various forms until I began to pay serious attention to their content. At this time I was living on the site of an ancient temple, dating back to pre-Roman times, with a strong classical presence involving Celtic, Roman and Greek worship. The local goddess, presiding over hot springs, was a deity of therapy, opening and closing, blessing and cursing. She was, in short, an Underworld goddess. My own meditations and spiritual work in a house on the site seemed to open certain deep levels of awareness, represented by the goddess and by an underground temple in a cavern with a central pool.

The repeated image of a cavern below the temple site was, at first, meaningless, as the site would have originally been a swamp due to the copious hot springs flooding out into the nearby river. Yet on an inner level there were caves. I dreamt about them, and saw them in my meditation. I could not deny their persistent appearance, so I decided to explore them further.

Having taken this step of commitment, I began to work with the imagery that had repeatedly declared itself . . . climbing down a flight of steps into a dark cavern with a pool in the centre. On the opposite side of the cavern was another flight of steps leading to an alcove, and in this a dark female figure stood. This type of dream and subsequent visualization may have a materialist psychological value, but as a magical or spiritual experience it brings powerful energies and changes of consciousness that are not admitted in modern therapy.

After working with the scene described in waking visualization, I had a new and quite violent frightening dream. In this dream, which I shall never forget, I was shown a small wooden door in an earthy bank or hillside. A symbol was carved upon the door and as I looked at it, a voice spoke directly into my ear, from behind my shoulder where I could not see the speaker.

'This is a way that no one has taken for a long time . . . are you willing to take it?' I said yes, and immediately the door opened. I passed inside and was instantly hurled down a long stone-lined tunnel at great speed. I seemed to turn inside out, as if everything, every aspect and fragment of my being, physical, mental, emotional, spiritual, was reversed. I felt great fear. I tumbled and travelled through the tunnel very rapidly, in a confused and unhappy state, with everything that I had assumed to be valuable inverted, challenged, turned upside down and inside out, including my own meagre insights and inner work. I felt reduced to the barest essence of life, and was afraid that I would die. Suddenly I fell to a great depth and emerged into a brilliant light. Then I awakened, sweating, shaking, exalted and terrified. It took me several days to balance the impact of the dream, and I knew that something important had happened, even though I was not fully aware of what it might be.

Now when I pursued my visualization of the cavern and the dark female figure, I found it was possible to cross the intervening space and approach Her. She was the goddess of the Underworld, the Black Isis. A long series of communications and teachings followed, from unseen but recognizable and distinct sources, mainly during sleep.

During this period I gained insights into a range of traditional themes that had been long preserved in ancient ballads that were always regarded as 'magical' but which no one had ever considered to have a true initiatory or transformative effect. These were not quaint olde-worlde relics from an ignorant past but the ancestral lore of the Northern and Western Underworld tradition.

I had volunteered for the Underworld Initiation, and was now working through the effects of my terrifying journey. With each successive
visit it became easier, more balanced, less turbulent, and eventually I
realized that a right of presence had been conferred upon me. I had a
right to open certain doors and pass within, and was able to take others
there and back again. Eventually I learned the relationship between
inherent ancestral (or what we might today call genetic) potential and its
realized awakened state. This awakening was the Communion with the
Ancestors, to which we shall return in later chapters.

The Faery Realm

One of the best ways to communicate the faery realm in a book is
through relating personal experiences. My own experience of this world
and inhabitants, and those of groups of people whom I have led in and
out of the faery realm in empowered visualization, will, I hope, convey
far more of its true nature than lengthy discussions of theory, folklore or
esoteric philosophy.

While the folk traditions are essential in establishing a historical and
collective basis for the faery contacts and the techniques known to our
ancestors, they cannot and do not apply fully today, for our culture is
radically different from that of only seventy years ago. A balance must
be found between esoteric lore, folklore and a direct modern experience
of, and interaction with, the faery realm and its inhabitants. The practical
experience and interaction is everything . . . without it the ancestral lore
is valueless other than as a store of curiosities. Nor will too much space
be wasted here on any argument for, or 'proof' of, the existence of the
faery realm and other regions of the Underworld. Anyone working with
the exercises and techniques suggested in the later chapters can prove or
disprove for themselves. The personal and group experiences that are
drawn upon through this book are not offered as 'proof' of anything.
They are simply extracts or short summaries from whatever happened
when modern people began to explore the Underworld or faery realm.

Before relating my own experiences, I feel that I should give some
initial information on techniques in modern group workings involving
the faery realm. This operational material is developed more fully in the
second part of this book. These modern empowered visualizations or
journeys have been undertaken between 1978 and today, with groups
ranging in size from three or four to fifty, and on a few occasions with as
many as one hundred and fifty. The groups gathered in England,
Scotland, Wales, Ireland and America. Faery working in America is

distinct from that in Britain and Ireland. There are also differences between the various regions of the British Isles, but with a general unity.

I should begin by summarizing the principal features of group workings. The group was generally given some background to the faery tradition, and if necessary some preliminary visualization and energy work with Sacred Space and the Seven Directions.[8] This preliminary attuning of consciousness and energy is important in working with the faery realm, for our ancestral lands (such as prehistoric Ireland) were aligned according to an idealized North, East, South and West, attuned to the Four Elements and unified by a central fifth zone.[9] This pattern is found in visualizing and energy work in our later chapters.

The alignment of the state, city or sacred land is found in many ancient cultures worldwide; planetary directions are considered important to the health of the land, and people of certain qualities and functions are ideally located in the four quarters, all harmonized by a central fifth. If we work with this elemental and directional pattern, our experiences of the faery realm are enhanced and balanced. Without this primal world-pattern, the faery experiences tend to be less defined, and potentially diffuse or even imbalanced. Experiments working with groups using visualization with and without the prior attuning of Sacred Space has persuaded me of this, though interestingly there is no overt declaration of the Directions in the faery realm itself.

The orientation of the Directions and Elements is valuable for us both before and after encounters in the Underworld, but not always used there in its own right. It is as if the energies need to be patterned before entry and realigned on emerging, but are loosened and transformed during the encounters themselves.

After the background and some working with Directions and Elements, plus the idea of the sacred land in ancient cultures, the group would be led into faeryland, through guided visualization. This is a specific technique in which the narrative of the visualization is empowered by the narrator, who must have personal experience of the faery realm, and of the energy patterns of Sacred Space. Some examples of visualizations are found in Part Two of this book, and are also recorded on cassette.[10]

After working with several groups in different locations, many regular features became noticeable. People with no connections with one another and in different lands frequently reported similar experiences during the faery Underworld visualizations. I shall leave out those more obvious similarities deriving from the imagery and themes of the tradition, and focus upon a few unusual features.

The first is that of prevision or even pre-empting. Group members frequently reported seeing aspects of the visualization before hearing them described by me, and of reaching certain locations, meeting certain beings, before I had taken the group to these points of encounter. Usually the prevision was shortly before the narration itself, as if certain individuals were one or two steps ahead in a group journey but still with the group. In other examples, more rare, some people moved far ahead of the group, yet remained within the scene that I was yet to describe to them, often having encounters and reaching locations before the main group. In contrast very few people reported a visualizing experience that departed far from the narrative or that wandered into unknown zones, encounters, fantasies or absurdities.

Another feature of faery realm visualizations was that the entire group would usually reach a specific location as described, but individual experiences within that location might be coloured in unusual ways. These variations occurred naturally without departing from the scene or losing the general development of the group encounter, narrative, journey or intent.

The faery inhabitants, for example, would generally appear in a coherent manner to all group members, yet one or two individuals in a group often had their visions and experiences coloured in vivid imagery and personalities. This is partly because faery beings draw upon our own imagination and store of expressions for their presentation. They tend to model themselves upon patterns that we can understand, and in modes of communication with which we are familiar. This is not, however, the same as saying that they are fantasies drawn from wishful thinking, for apart from individual coloration, they preserve a strict and recognisable identity and behaviour. It is not possible, for example, to force a faery being, in empowered visualization, to change shape or aspect into something alien to its nature. Nor is it possible to force communication with beings that do not wish it, though you may be aware of their presence. We shall return to these subjects again.

The broad pattern of the faery world and its occupants is preserved in the collective imagery of tradition, but individual examples and encounters are modified out of this collective imagery into various expressions. Through all this run some fundamental themes, entities and energies, which are not transformed by human imagination or contact but act instead to transform us.

My own encounters with the faery realm and people have been many, both in group workings and as an individual. The most significant encounters have come as spontaneous events, even as surprises. The most important (though not the first) encounter was in 1982 in Scotland. This recovered and regenerated an entire level of awareness and memory concerning the faery realms and ancestral traditions. It was to lead eventually to my new edition of *The Secret Commonwealth of Elves, Fauns and Fairies (Robert Kirk: Walker Between Worlds*, Element Books, 1990). Although eight years passed before the book appeared, time means little in a faery context.

This 1982 event was not my first faery realm or faery being encounter, but was the one that opened out the experience for me. It also helped to bring alive my own ability to lead others in and out of the faery realm. As this event has played a major part in certain aspects of my own life and work, it is perhaps worth recounting in some detail. Much of the material in this book derives from the strange encounter that I am about to describe, though my Underworld experiences began, as I have briefly outlined above, some years before. While the faery realm is in the Underworld, the Underworld itself is far more than the faery realm alone.

In the summer of 1982 I travelled to Scotland to visit a friend who was studying mysticism at Stirling University. Although I am a Scot, I had lived in England for most of my life; this visit was to prove a homecoming in many ways. I was to visit Stirling and the home region of the Reverend Robert Kirk who studied the Gaelic faery tradition in the seventeenth century. The invitation had been given by Deirdre Green, later to be Doctor Green, author of *Gold in the Crucible* (Element Books, 1989). She took me to Aberfoyle, where Kirk's grave may be seen, and where a local faery tradition involving him persists to the present day.

In brief the local tradition reports that Kirk was taken into faeryland, and that although his body was found upon a nearby faery hill, this was not a true death. Attempts were made as late as the twentieth century to recover Kirk from the faery realm, where tradition insisted that he still dwelt. I was aware of this story, but not particularly responsive to it. My enthusiasm diminished when, with Deirdre and another friend, John Hicks, we found that the faery hill at Aberfoyle was conveniently marked by a trail of red mushroom-shaped signs for presumed tourists.

The hill itself was wooded and wild ... we were the only people there despite the markings and the path set out along the local 'faery trail'. We climbed to the top of the hill and then individually found quiet locations to sit and meditate. I sat by a rowan tree, a major tree in faery tradition, and used by the Gaels as a protection against malice, for guarding gateways and thresholds.

I sat and meditated for some time, feeling peaceful and quiet, but with no overt faery contact. Nor did I expect one, as I was quite cynical about the entire matter and had, anyway, closed myself to that part of my ancestral heritage for some years. Just as I was about to stand up and leave, I suddenly found I was communing with someone. He was a short man, fairly plump, who declared himself to be Robert Kirk, fully alive in the faery realm. The communication came suddenly and was quite a surprise. This person seemed quite human and normal, but had a curious energetic quality about him. Without any preamble he told me of an entire group of men (specifically males) who were in the faery realm, including people from Celtic tradition and from other quite unlikely (and, to my mind at the time, faintly ridiculous) sources and time periods. This group was called the order or brotherhood of 'Justified Men'. I only report what I experienced, and make no claims to represent or understand this group of mortals apparently dwelling in the immortal faery world. The tradition, however, is one that occurs in various forms worldwide, though I was not aware of this until some years later.

After describing this group, who are all people who had *physically* translated into the faery realm, Robert Kirk made a strong invitation for me to join them. The sensation was of a doorway opening from this world to another, and that I could physically step through. I stood to take that step and as I raised my foot I heard, in the distance, a horn blowing. Let me be precise; it was a car horn, and its sound summoned me back to my responsibilities in the present place and time. I did not step through. But I do not wonder what would have occurred if I had stepped through, physically, into the faery realm, as I have visited it often in various ways during the last ten years.

That night, staying in the region, I had vivid dreams in which Robert Kirk and certain allied faery beings educated me in faery metaphysics, philosophy and the art of the Seven Directions. Much of this education was to appear in my later books. I was also taken, in dream or vision, on a lengthy journey around Scotland to many powerful locations, some of which I was to visit physically in later years, recognizing them suddenly from this intense dream communication.

Perhaps I should state, at this point, that I am not concerned over the so-called identity source or nature of this sequence of communications. I see no reason why it should not have been Robert Kirk, especially as other people have experienced similar contact with him in the region. Various people claim to have contacted him upon inner or imaginal dimensions in meditation and visualization.

The significance of the encounter, I believe, is that I had not studied for it or looked for it; indeed, I was sceptical of anything happening. I realized later that my scepticism masked a deep but uncertain connection with the faery realm, something inherited from my Celtic ancestors and based in part upon obscured childhood memories of Otherworld contact. The value was that a mass of lore, teaching, specific workable material came out of the contact, material that I have since developed for work with other people.

So Kirk or not, something happened that involved the faery realm and the ways in and out of it, for myself and for others. My opinion is that it was indeed the Reverend Robert Kirk, and some of the techniques that I learned during my time under his tuition put me into contact with other people, historical humans, living in the faery realm. Many of my previously held, rather glib modern interpretations of the faery tradition as quaint folklore were radically changed by this adventure.

During my editing and commentary upon Kirk's *Secret Commonwealth of Elves, Fauns and Fairies*, undertaken in 1989, I felt his pervasive advisory presence, but no direct contact of the dramatic and concentrated sort that I had experienced in his native territory. Tragically Deirdre died in a car crash in 1990, shortly before the publication of that book; without her persistence and loving friendship years before, I might never have made that journey to Scotland, met with Kirk, and so proceeded in and out of the faery realm. I owe much to her.

2. The Faery People

There are two well-established interpretations of the nature of the faery people, with a number of variations according to religion or culture. The modern materialist understanding is that they are inherent, either passively or actively, within the psyche . . . they have no independent entity as actual living beings other than in human consciousness. The traditional understanding is that they are independent beings, of several different kinds, many of which are close to the race of humans but not identical to them.

The pre-materialist or metaphysical view of the faery races is often confused in modern interpretation by the repeated reports of the presence of deceased relatives and ancestors, and human beings who have been *physically* translated to the faery realm, either by faery beings through acts of intent or by accident at sacred sites and other power locations in the land. If we simply read or listen to traditional accounts, we find no such confusion, as the three classes are clearly defined and generally understood in folklore. The problems arise with materialist interpretation, determined to fit everything into a psychological model based upon superstition or ignorance. In truth the faery tradition is consistent and coherent, even after centuries of religious and social oppression.

Within the psychological approach we find a number of themes, according to the schools of psychology supported: the faery beings are sexual images; they are 'archetypes' such as those of the classical gods and goddesses; they are embodiments and projected images of our fear of the unknown; they are the remnants of an old nature religion; they are the collective superstitious fantasies of a pre-materialist humanity groping towards the enlightenment of a psychological approach to consciousness. And so forth.

Our traditional inheritance is vast and complex. In orthodox religion the faery beings are, not surprisingly, given credence but are regarded as evil or at best, frivolous and distracting influences. With the death throes of orthodox Christianity in Western culture, a materialist approach has prevailed in many religions and the existence of other orders of being, non-human, non-organic, is simply ignored or denied.

The old-style priests who sought to keep their congregations away from faery contact were only too well aware of the power of the ancestral traditions; they did not regard faery lore or Underworld customs as fantasy or mere ignorance. Interestingly, we find reports of priests in Celtic regions such as Scotland or Ireland with the second sight, with knowledge of and communion with faery beings; as recently as the early years of the twentieth century W. Y. Evans Wentz, the author of *The Fairy Faith in Celtic Countries*,[3] found a range of such Christian priests, Protestant and Catholic, who were attuned to the traditions. So even in orthodox terms, there is an interaction between religion and the faery faith, in a positive rather than dogmatic or superstitious sense. This subject is discussed in more depth in *Power Within The Land*.

Much faery lore contains, undeniably, the beliefs of pagan religion. So interpretation of faery beings and their nature will vary from land to land for historical and cultural reasons; it will also vary because faery beings are related closely to the land itself, a more subtle environmental subject to which we shall return in other chapters. But from classical times to the folklore of the twentieth century, we find a line of continuity regarding the nature of these beings, a continuity which crosses historical and cultural boundaries. This traditional inheritance might be summarized as follows:

1. There is a race or order of non-organic, 'immaterial' or spiritual beings which is close to humanity.
2. This race is attuned to the land and, like humanity, varies from land to land but has an overall unity.
3. They may communicate with and relate to humans, particularly in the context of the vitality of the land or environment.
4. They are said to *mirror* humanity in many ways, just as the faery world is said to be the mirror image or primal image of our own.
5. A fifth concept, which I feel has been passed over or ignored in modern studies of folklore and faery tradition, is that the faery beings will adapt themselves to whatever they find in our

imaginations. Alternatively we could say that our minds form images for us as a result of fairy contact, but that the images are variable and malleable.

These words are my own, of course, but in major sources such as Robert Kirk, we find the same idea expressed in ethical terms. He says that if our souls are pure then our contact with the faery race is beneficial and harmonious, but if there is 'a demur' upon the soul, the beneficial contact will depart. He also states that a negative or unhealthy contact will mirror the qualities of the human being. Whatever we take with us into faeryland may reflect through whoever we meet and whatever we bring out. But the situation is not static, as the faery encounter is transformative: the 'secret' art was to take what you wanted to be changed into the faery realm, offer it up, and come back with whatever was freely given to you in return.

Kirk also describes, throughout his text, the fact that the faery beings take on temporary shapes to communicate with us. They will take the form of a loved one or someone recently dead to convey messages through imagery, concerning matters that have happened or which will happen. Celtic seership was closely involved with the interpretation of a large collection of typical or systematic images, the form and meaning of which were taught through oral instruction between seers, preserved for many centuries. As a rule this symbolic instruction was for images seen with the second sight, and may not apply in such detail to commonplace faery sightings on a day-to-day basis.

According to Kirk, specific images, forming an alphabet or known series of units, such as the type and amount of clothing upon a faery being, the stance, approach or departure of a faery co-walker, and other symbolic displays, were specifically produced by the faery beings, and often drawn from the imaginative stock of humans. This is an interesting teaching, for it fits with a number of typical traditional magical arts worldwide. In such traditions the initiate is trained in a stock of images, symbols, patterns, movements and so forth. These eventually enable communication between human and non-human entities.

The Kabbalistic Tree of Life, much used in Western magic, is a classic model of symbolic patterns, glyphs, images and the attribution of sacred letters: this is comparable to the system used among the Gaelic seers, and the rune magic of Northern magicians and shamans. In Renaissance magic we find very sophisticated developments of this idea, such as the Enochian alphabet of Dr John Dee, taught directly by spirits for specific communication and invocation. Dee's researches also involved seership, through the use of a crystal and a seer, Edward Kelly, who perceived and reported but did not necessarily understand what he was seeing.

My own experience causes me to feel that through his various comments, Robert Kirk has given us a very true account of faery contact, although it is obviously in the language of his day and certainly inhibited and coloured by the religious tone of the seventeenth century. The favourable comparisons that we can make between Kirk's material and folklore and magical tradition worldwide are firm evidence that he reported an active tradition.

In many ways *The Secret Commonwealth* was a very bold document to produce at a time when the Puritans were still burning people accused of witchcraft or, in attested contemporary cases such as that of Major Weir and his sister, who learned weaving from the Faery Queen, consorting with faery beings and working magic. Kirk's book was not, of course, published for centuries after his death and was intended, it seems, only for private circulation amongst clerics.

If we set aside for the moment the presence of ancestors and human beings in the faery realm and concentrate upon the nature of the faery beings themselves, Kirk's report, from Gaelic tradition of the seventeenth century, holds the key to something important. The faery beings will appear and communicate according to what is in our own imagination . . . but they are not products of the imagination.

Kirk describes them as being of a chamaeleon-like nature, changing shape and colour, light and insubstantial, made of a cloud of vital substance. This accords very well with a moving description reported by Evans Wentz from a famous Irish seer and mystic. The source was A. E. (George Russell) whose remarkable writings and faery paintings are essential studies for anyone working with the faery tradition.

In my own work and group work using visualization both in private workshops and at outdoor faery sites, there has been a regular tendency for faery contacts to draw certain patterns from the imagination of the humans. There is a distinct difference between this interaction and simple association, fantasy or projection of preconditioned images, none of which involve the presence of other intelligences.

Perhaps the most obvious and repeatedly reported difference is the will and motivation of the faery beings; they may indeed appear clothed in an imaginative form that you recognize, and may communicate according to patterns and rhythms of speech or imagery that you yourself would use, but they do not do your bidding. In many examples of encounters the faery will is very strong indeed, and many unexpected dramatic events occur. This is another feature of faery encounters often reported in the old tradition, that humans must reach an accord and a balanced relationship with faery beings and not get carried away, either literally or metaphorically.

THE NATURE OF THE FAERY BEINGS

The nature of faery beings is well described in tradition, with oral sources making clear distinctions between faery people, the spirits of the dead or ancestors in the faery realm, and those who have been taken or voluntarily remain as living humans in the faery realm.

Some further information from esoteric tradition, also handed down through the centuries but preserved in a more narrow line of communication, is available. This is supported by the insights of modern individual and group work using techniques described in this book. Several items of knowledge recur frequently, so are worth presenting briefly here.

1.   The faery beings are often discovered to be collective entities or hive-beings. This is a valuable but frequently confused idea. There are various orders or collectives of faery beings, just as there are several races of humans. One of the major differences between the faery beings and humans is that the faeries are collective or hive-beings in most cases.

The various orders of faery being have a hive-like nature: communicate with one and you communicate with all members of that hive or tribe. This uniform intelligence is the means by which many of the powerful interactions between humans and faery beings occur, and we often assume that we are dealing with an individual in the human sense, when we are communicating with a collective. It is for this reason that in direct visualization and empowered workings entering the faery realm through imagery, we first relate to the King and Queen. They represent the ultimate polarity of all faery beings, regardless of their nature, hive, tribe or order. An example of such visualization is found on page 78.

In reality there may be a number of 'kings and queens' of various orders, but this collective is ultimately subsumed under the powerful beings that appear to our imaginative vision in the traditional form of Faery King and Faery Queen. Just as a queen bee is not a ruler in a political sense, we should not expect the faery rulers to be hierarchical or political. Kingship and queenship are qualities and inherent powers, not titles or authoritarian roles.

Not all faery beings interconnect, however, for the different orders may also relate to one another without necessarily sharing a hive consciousness. In one sense certain orders of faery beings are the elementals of medieval and Renaissance magic, for they are not comprised of all five Elements as humans are. The Elements are shown in their holistic cycle and relationship in Figure 2. Each Element has within itself a configuration of the others, and so on in a pattern of perpetual relativity and mathematical attraction. This pattern making, well known and openly taught in the magical traditions, has recently been 'discovered' by orthodox mathematics through the use of computers, producing so-called 'chaos' images . . . which are in fact resonant or reiterative elemental patterns inherent in nature. Seers and meditators have been observing and participating in such patterns for millennia but today, of course, the computer 'discovers' them afresh and 'proves' them.

Such patterns are an important key to the true nature of faery beings, just as they are the key to the power of the Elements. Faery beings, however, may have a limited relative cycle of Elements and can only balance by merging with other beings that have the missing elemental energy.

This is the heart of the ancient magic of faery partners or marriages: a human will find his or her weakest Element strengthened and vitalized by relationship with a faery being: the faery being finds the potential fivefold Elemental pattern through relationship with a human. To paraphrase one of the oldest traditions concerning relationships between humans and faery beings, we have the potential to *redeem* them, to give them a spiritual element or constituent which they do not have, while they have the potential to *regenerate* us, to realign our imbalanced energies in harmony with primal images and environmental and planetary consciousness. According to Kirk, the Celtic seers taught that all that existed was alive, with every form having other living beings upon or within it. Today we call this holism; energies and entities interacting within one another.

2. Faery beings do not have the emotion of human love. They are often described as without emotions, though this does not imply coldness or callousness, simply a lack of human feelings. The deeper spiritual powers are known to faery beings, and love upon a universal level is inherent within them. One of the major interchanges between humanity and the faery beings is upon our human level of emotions and personal feelings. . . the exchange of personal love and affection between the sexes, and between parents and children. This theme is often found in tradition, in the context of tales and songs about faery lovers and stolen children.

It also masks a deeper wisdom teaching, that selfless love is more powerful than selfish. In Fiona Macleod's *Immortal Hour*, which contains

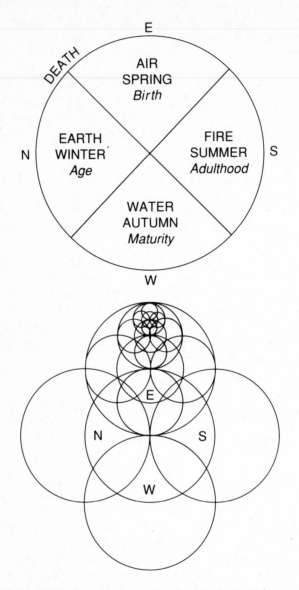

Figure 2(a) The Five Elements: *Air, Fire, Water, Earth, Spirit* or *Central Being*.

Figure 2(b) The Elements are relative states and patterns of energy/consciousness. The fivefold pattern reiterates in each Element, and in all relative Elemental patterns.

many fragments of faery lore woven into an Edwardian Celtic-twilight drama, the greatest power is described as *love at peace*, far more potent than *love aflame with all desire*.

3.   Faery companions mirror certain attributes of the human that they are drawn towards, often complementing something lacking in the human, just as the human complements something lacking in the faery being. One of the most dangerous energetic patterns is where we mistakenly generate human sexual attraction or interaction with a faery being. In tradition such faery lovers are said to be inordinately demanding: this is due to the lack of human feeling and simple affection. Sexual links with faery beings were frequently the subject of complaints and warnings from the Christian priesthood, not merely as dogma but as direct result of the day-to-day beliefs and practices of ordinary people.

4.   Time cycles within the faery world are different from ours. The commonly reported theme is that a short period of time in the faery realm may be centuries in the human world. This is interesting in a number of ways, not the least of which is the cycle of the last 300 years in which we have grown apart from the faery beings. Perhaps this time is very brief, a few 'months' or 'days', in their realm. But as there is no Moon or Sun in the faery realm, there is no rotational clock of nights, days or lunar and solar cycles. The light within the Earth is direct light, that of spirit living within matter. A better way to express this in written words would be *spirit-living-matter*.

The other interesting pattern inherent in the question of subjective time in the faery realm is that a faery contact may have also contacted your ancestors. Traditionally faery communication, second sight and the ability to consciously enter the faery realm often run in families. A faery contact that comes to you may also have been the contact of your ancestors; the faery beings do not age or suffer illness but they may eventually die, according to reports such as those of Robert Kirk. Other more religiously prejudiced reports suggest that they are truly immortal but lament being unable to die and return to another realm or world from which they were cast out. We will return to this important idea in *Power Within The Land*.

THE TYPES AND APPEARANCES OF FAERY BEINGS

The popular image of the faery beings is that of the sentimental Victorians: cosy little gossamer creatures with insect wings. No such beings are reported from tradition, in which the people of the *sidh* are generally said to be of human size or taller. The many traditional reports concerning small faery beings, little men and women dressed in various colours, carry the half-apologetic, half-condescending approach that ordinary people often took towards folklore collectors.

The folklore collectors were of a different class, usually authoritarian figures as far as common folk were concerned. Often they were priests or scholars from a very orthodox religious background: little wonder that the sources were cautious. Yes, I have often seen *them*, but of course they are only little'. 'I never saw any myself, of course, but my cousin saw some once and said that they were very small. . .' It is interesting to note that such dismissive descriptions are not found in Kirk, the earliest detailed direct account of Gaelic faery lore, in which faery beings are of human stature.

The little sprite with Victorian paedophiliac implications, white childish limbs, short gossamer dresses and so forth, is unknown in the faery realm. Such creatures seem to be the products of repressed sexual fantasy in the nineteenth and early twentieth centuries. Some of the implications of this are found in Maureen Duffy's hilarious (but self-consciously serious) book *The Erotic World of Faery*[11] in which the author carries some obvious conclusions to ludicrous extremes.

It is interesting to find that when working with modern groups in empowered visualization, very few small, winged beings are reported. In group workings we might find one or two reports of such beings, with the great majority reporting encounters with beings of human shape and size, and a range of other shapes and sizes. This seems to me to be significant, as we might expect modern visualizers to produce pretty little faeries from their own imaginations, but in the heightened circumstances of the Underworld such images seldom appear. We shall return shortly to a few descriptions of beings that frequently arise in group workings, usually in the context of faery allies or companions. But before we do so, a word about clothing.

FAERY FASHIONS

It seems clear both from tradition and from modern work that the fashions of the faery realm are heterogeneous. Working with modern groups who have had little or no priming in what the faery beings might wear, we find very consistent results, in keeping with oral tradition for centuries. The costumes are of all types and all time periods: many are human costumes of previous centuries. Others are weird, to us, often extremely bizarre.

The exotic dress of certain faery beings is remarkably similar to the costumes described in early Irish sagas, which seem to preserve a poetic tradition handed down from the Bronze Age, as weapons are frequently of bronze or bone.[12] We find that a modern group with no previous experience of such imagery will describe beings wearing armour and costumes just as they are described in ancestral Irish texts. The texts themselves were transcriptions of much earlier oral epic poetry, preserved from a pagan culture dating back to pre-Celtic times, but primarily of the Celtic 'heroic' type.

In this class we find warriors, beings both male and female, of a tall stature, thin, often with strange coloured and exotically styled hair. They wear armour of bone, including fine scale armour, often seeming like fish skins and scales; they carry ornate weapons of bronze, stone, bone and wood. These beings form one of the hive-groups that seem prominent in visions of the faery realm. They are, typically, under the collective awareness of the Faery King and Queen. Within this class or entity we also find occasional human and ex-human beings, who seem to be of the order of faery warriors but not bound by the collective consciousness. This relationship is found in many of the faery orders or classes of being which have human or ex-human members and associates.

I feel that these beings represent the 'high' faery tradition and that the appearance derives from the original images of the people of the *sidhe* or Tuatha De Danann. In Irish tradition, the *Tuatha De Danann* appeared in the land, manifesting from another world or dimension, upon a sacred mountain. They came from four Otherworldly cities, located at each of the cardinal directions (see Chapter 6). As faery beings take temporary shape from images in the collective consciousness of humanity (as far as we are concerned), these entities present to us the collective tradition of the ancient world. Other beings in costumes of later periods represent collective images from other human contacts and interactions.

The ancient groupings seem to form a large proportion of the occupants of the faery realm, and we might expect this as they are from a time when there was no separation between human and faery beings, and no religious persecution, as the period was pre-Christian.

We also find various faery groups in costumes and appearances presenting the noble cultures of the past: they appear to have a courtly pattern. There are harpers, pipers, warriors, heralds, young men and maidens, stewards, story-tellers, and so forth. All the social apparatus and castes of bygone centuries. We need to consider these appearances in terms of *function* rather than of romantic escapism. The function is displayed by the image or dress, but the being remains true to itself or its hive-descent.

STRANGE AND STRANGER BEINGS

There are also many other non-organic and non-human types in the faery realm. These are, once again, reported with an interesting consistency by modern groups with whom I have worked. In all cases the group is not briefed to expect any particular type of being, as this is intentionally left open. During empowered visualizations, such as the one in Chapter 5 in which we enter a faery hall in the Underworld and meet faery allies and companions, a range of strange beings are reported. These are consistent in many ways with traditional material. Some typical examples would be as follows:

Allies of Great Size

People are often approached by potential allies of considerable size, which have a more or less human appearance. One group member typically reported that his nose reached to his ally's chest, and that the being was powerful, slow and barely communed other than through simple actions. Another reported a large hearty human-like character who offered him friendship and protection. In my own earliest faery realm experiences I acquired a very powerful ally, before I had explored the tradition in any depth. I am not, unfortunately, able to describe this being in detail, as I have never seen it fully, only in glimpses.

Furthermore, in a typical faery compact, if I named or described the ally this would be a breach of some kind of trust or exchange that I do not fully understand. If the being was publicly described, it would disappear. This theme is found repeatedly in folk tales of faery helpers whose names, natures and appearances must be kept secret. In some tales those who talk lose their allies or companions, while in others those who had a sight of the faery realm and subsequently reveal their ability to see it are stricken blind by faery beings.

When I first realized that I had acquired a faery companion, I was shocked by what I saw of its appearance and, until I realized that it was helpful to me, quite worried by its occasional presence. All I can say is that it is larger than a man, but manlike in shape, with silver scales or armour. These powerful large beings invariably act as protectors in emergencies, and may do nothing for years until they are truly needed.

My understanding is that they simply observe and slowly learn of our world in exchange for the potential of their protection should it be necessary. There are probably other reasons and exchanges that I am not aware of.

Many people report allies which are theriomorphic ... comprising jointly animal and human characteristics. These frequently include beings with hawks' heads, for they are an important part of the faery-human tradition and also represent an ancient god-form.[13] Most faery beings are reported as having unusual eyes, often the eyes of an animal or bird, or eyes of startling colour and perceptive qualities. When we approach the Faery King and Queen in empowered workings, they have the ability to *see through* and summarize a human being in a glance.

Bodies of Light

Another typical reported form is that of amorphous bodies of light: this presentation was often reported outdoors, as if this is the raw energetic appearance of a faery being without the substance of human imagination from which to draw shape. The famous Irish mystic A. E. (George Russell) described beings of this sort from his own experience, and their luminous quality is found in his faery paintings.

Another aspect of this is found in visualization, particularly group work in which the development of the visualization and Underworld contact is guided. Various people in groups that I have led in and out of the faery realm have reported that certain parts of the experience dissolve into less defined images. This is not a weakening or loss of concentration, for people feel it to be the most intense part of the experience.

In many examples, individuals found that rather than seeing a group of faery beings directly, with individual bodies as broadly defined in the story or visualized narrative (see page 78), they saw a collection of patterns, flowing light, and amorphous shapes. Despite this lack of form, the feeling of presence and power was intense.

Dissolution of form is a classic meditational experience, in which our consciousness makes a direct energy exchange or communion, beyond the need for form. Conversely it may, on occasions, be regarded as a type of limitation or protection, something which is frequently taught in older primal traditions that work with spirit companions of any sort. The inability to see the contacts is regarded as a protecting filter, out of our own psyche, our own conditioning. With practice, with specific techniques, it may be removed and we may see the companions direct.

A typical experience is sighting contacts or allies for a brief flash, or out of peripheral vision, but not directly. The Gaelic seers trained themselves to look without blinking or refocusing the eyes ('twinkling' as Robert Kirk called it). This fixity of stare is the physical counterpart to an inner focusing and ability to look directly into the Otherworld or Underworld.

LAWS OF THE FAERY REALM

The faery realm exists according to laws that are 'opposite' to our own. We seem to have cause and effect (popularly and inaccurately known as *karma*) but the faery realm has no such causes, no effects as we understand them ... it resonates beyond such cycles of energy. The most obvious difference, well attested in folklore and tradition, is the different time cycle in the faery realm. A short time there may be centuries in the human world.

As humans we feel ourselves to be bound by the cycles of Moon and Sun, and more subtly but no less powerfully by the cycles of stars. The faery realm is not lit by Sun or Moon but by an inherent light within the land itself. It also draws light from the stars within the Earth, which are mirror images of the patterns seen in our own sky. There is a subtle connection here between astrology and the faery realm, for the pattern of our birth chart is dependent upon *location*, upon the place within the land in which we are born. This resonance is imprinted in our life pattern, or synchronous with it, dependent upon your point of view. However we interpret this harmony or holism of patterns between human life cycle and the stellar configurations relative to our horizon, it is the *point upon the land* that decides the pattern of the natal chart, when combined with the time of birth.

Time, Space and Energy are the three relative powers that provide a stellar matrix for our life pattern. Space involves location and relative position upon the surface of the planet. This also gives us our Underworld or faery contact, for the faery realm mirrors the location and stellar pattern of our birth place. The absence of Sun and Moon in the faery realm shows the absence of certain human characteristics in the faery people ... we can give to them certain energies which they lack, just as they can give to us certain energies which we lack. Unified, we make a fusion of perfect being and the primal planet. In the next chapter we will begin to explore means to enable our fusion, to reveal the Light within the Earth.

3. Going and Returning

A Short Summary of the Basics

There are many ways in and out of the Underworld, and many realms and beings within it. The real differences that we find between cultures, and how they define and describe the Underworld, are *ancestral* and *environmental*. Different lands have different types of Underworld. All, however, merge together in the primal planet, the power realm within the Earth. At its deepest level this inner-Earth contains the stars: the planet is the universe. We reach a universal vision through environmental and ancestral traditions, by passing into the land itself. But by doing so we also extend and amplify our consciousness within our own bodies, bringing altered awareness and specific transformations of energy through Underworld techniques and encounters.

For the present we can bypass mythic and historical continuity and the vast oral traditions upon which this book is based (though we will return to them from time to time). If we reduce all of the collective inheritance of Underworld traditions and the specific so-called 'secret teachings' down to a set of straightforward techniques and exercises, what would we have?

A simple summary of the basic Underworld techniques and experiences, directly available to any modern individual or group, would be as follows:

1. *Preparation* We prepare for the Underworld experience in meditation. This usually involves a period of silence and stillness, in which attention is withdrawn from outer habitual or conditioned patterns. This first stage of preparation is essential and should not be bypassed or skipped through hastily. Without the preparation of stillness and silence,

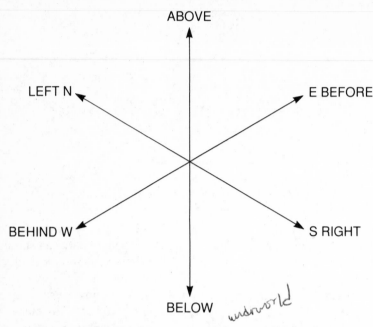

ABOVE

LEFT N

E BEFORE

BEHIND W

S RIGHT

BELOW   *underworld*

Figure 3 The Seven Directions. *Human*: 1 Above/2 Below/3
Within: 4 Before/5 Behind/6 Right/7 Left. *Environmental*: 1
Stars (above)/2 Underworld (Below)/3 Land (surface): 4
East/5 South/6 West/7 North.

your Underworld experience will not be clear, and may become
confused with impressions from your regular outer life.

A second stage of preparation which has proved effective, particularly with group working, is to dedicate and attune to Sacred Space. This
involves being aware of the Seven Directions (North, East, South, West,
Above, Below, Within). The planetary directions are attuned to the Four
Elements, Four Seasons and other attributes within the holism of the
living land and planet. These are shown in Figure 3. This second stage
also works as a long-term realignment of awareness, which we may
continue to develop for a lifetime.

The more we attune to the harmonized directions and energies, the
more effective they become within ourselves, adjusting many of our
conditioned imbalances and liberating coagulated or blocked energies.
The patterns are those of the natural Directions of the planet, and have a
powerful effect upon our own energy and consciousness when we work

7 directions

with them. It should be remembered that the southern and northern hemispheres of the planet mirror one another, with the Seasons and Directions polarized accordingly. In one mythic sense, the hemispheres are each others' Underworld, but only to the degree that they reflect stellar patterns. This deep mythic lore is explored in *Hamlet's Mill* by Giorgio de Santillana and Hertha von Dechend (Godine, Boston, 1977), a book which amply repays the effort of finding and reading a copy.

The Underworld experience is not, however, dependent upon working with the sacred Directions, and can be powerful and effective without this ongoing harmonization of the energies and elements. In modern practice I have found that even a day's work with the Directions will greatly enhance and harmonize Underworld experiences through visualization done on the following day. A basic work programme for various time scales (one day/two days/one week/one month/one year) is found in Appendix 1. These time scales have all been developed and experienced in regular work by myself and by various individuals and groups working with me or with Underworld techniques since 1978.

2. *Visualization* The simplest and most effective entry into the Underworld is through power of the imagination. We literally visualize ourselves into the realm below, those realms filled with the Light within the Earth. Such visualization consists of some obvious but important stages:

a) Visualizing a means of entry
b) Passing within
c) Travelling through the Underworld
d) Encountering specific places and people
e) Returning through the Underworld
f) Exiting, usually by the same means as the entry. The exit may vary and sometimes uses a different means to the entry.
g) Concluding and closing the visualization to return to regular outer awareness.

The seven basic units may be visualized in many different ways: a typical scenario might be:

a) A door
b) A flight of steps leading downwards
c) Emerging into a land within the Earth.
d) Travelling to locations that are predefined and meeting people there. (Usually we predefine the locations but not the encounters. More of this later.)
e) Retracing our steps through the land and back up the flight of steps.

f) Emerging into our starting location.
g) Dissolving the vision of the door and resuming normal patterns of
   thought and behaviour.

This simple process is greatly empowered by using traditional imagery.
There is a wealth of specific powerful imagery and information associated with the Underworld. It varies from land to land, and in this book
we are particularly concerned with the faery realm. Each land has its
own faery realm beneath it and within it, so although the examples used
in this book follow a Northern and Western faery and ancestral
tradition, the same techniques could be used with imagery and traditional beings from Southern and Eastern cultures.

   If we work very simply and follow the guidelines already established
by the traditions of our land, the Underworld experience is greatly
enhanced. The traditional themes and people, the faery narratives and
ancestral contacts enshrined within collective tales, songs and ceremonies are already a living part of the land and of our own relationship to
that land. Popular faery tales, once a central part of human experience
and shared imagery, are the remains of a tradition thousands of years
old, relating the connections between humanity and Otherworld beings.
Specifically faery tradition relates adventures involving the faery realm,
which is within and beneath the human realm.

DEVELOPING VISUALIZATIONS OF THE FAERY REALM

The Underworld contains various dimensions or realms, including the
faery realm, the ancestral realm (often part of the faery realm) and a
range of less accessible places and special groups or orders of beings.
We shall discover all of these and experience some contact with them as
we progress through the Underworld. For the present, let us concentrate
upon the faery realm, leaving the deeper zones to be explored more
fully in *Power Within The Land*.

   In oral tradition the potential encounters take various forms, ranging
from tales and songs to physical removal into the faery places beneath
the earth ... those halls filled with light. The physical translations are
direct experiences, but the themes, images and descriptions are embodied in traditional songs, stories and customs. These are the currency of
folklore that is well known from academic and anthropological studies
and from literary adaptations. With a small number of major exceptions,
most of the folklore material is too diffuse and confused for direct

modern use in visualization. This does not mean that it is ineffective, for it is very powerful, despite its cloak of childlike tale-telling.

To empower a traditional faery tale with its encounters and mysterious characters can be a profound and sometimes disturbing experience, but the empowerment usually needs some skill and previous work with the Underworld and faery traditions. There is a curious law, if we may use such a term, that comes into operation in working with raw traditional material from any culture. Someone who has experienced the deeper levels of the tradition, who has been into the realms described in the tales and songs, can make them work very powerfully indeed for others. Without the presence of such a person, the effect is diminished.

This is why the Underworld tradition is, in its original form, an initiatory one. To be initiated (i.e. started upon the journey) we have to work with someone who has already followed the path and returned again. Such people are not as rare as you might think, but we should still seek methods by which we can enter the Underworld and its realms and return again through imaginative work. The initiation then occurs automatically, through your own imaginative forces carrying you into the Underworld and back again. It is empowered by the people that you meet while you are in the Underworld, rather than by the presence of a human who has already entered and returned.

To develop visualizations, we need to first isolate some of the central patterns, the core of encounters, which are represented in the oral tradition of tales and songs. If we strip these of literary dressing and simplify them even further, we arrive at a set of people, powers and places. These purely functional aspects are the base for visualization.

If we work with traditional material, we need to identify the functions of the people, powers and places. Then we assemble a visualization based upon the most simple and direct versions of the tales, with no deviating from the central themes or fanciful dressing. *In short, we need to find who is in the vision, what effect and ability they have, and where they are located. We need to go there, meet the people concerned, and come out again.*

INITIATORY BALLADS

There are a few truly magical, truly initiatory ballads preserved in the oral tradition of the English language. By oral tradition we should understand a body of tales and songs handed down from generation to generation through family and collective memory. The transmission was through repetition and assimilation, and not through literature. There are significant interactions between oral tradition, the imagination and the use of imagery. This relationship, at the very core of consciousness, imagery and language, still applies to us today, a generation or more removed from the last phases of the vast oral traditions of our culture.

By such oral transmission we find that a wide range of tales and ballads survived well into the twentieth century, still containing the lore and imagery of much earlier times. The ballads always combine hauntingly powerful melodies with stark narrative and imagery. Among the thousands of traditional ballads known in English (though most are in Scots dialect or, in the American variants, Anglo-Irish-Scots amalgam), a small number contain magical or initiatory lore.

These few ballads have their counterparts in other European languages, and many have equivalents in most cultures all over the planet. For many years scholars, folklorists, enthusiasts, and nowadays revival pagans, have asserted that certain folk ballads are 'magical'. Some excellent academic criticism and comparative studies have been published and I would encourage you to read or at least hunt through as many of these source books as possible. But very few people have actually put the magic to the test. Are these ballads really magical, by which we must mean do they really transform us? Or are they merely quaint relics of a past culture, replete with supersition and archaic beliefs?

There are, in my opinion, based upon years of experience and inner work with the tradition, certain ballads that have a very powerful effect indeed upon our imagination, our energies, our overall being. This effect can be upon the purely receptive level of listening to and becoming enfolded within the ballads, or we can choose to move more deeply through our intent. In the Underworld tradition we find certain faery ballads of North-Western Europe (though I speak mainly for the British–American versions) to contain the seeds of a very ancient religion, that of the Dark Goddess.

They also preserve initiatory and transformative visions, which are in themselves both sources of inner power to enter the Underworld and descriptions of that Underworld or certain of its realms. Another small number of ballads preserve a fusion of Underworld imagery and early Christian symbolism. They carry the obscure but potent tradition of the Redeemer Within the Land: Christ within the Planet. We shall be examining this tradition in some depth in *Power Within the Land*, but it must be touched upon here, for it was preserved by ordinary people in their ballad singing.

It is interesting to find that the oral ballads of Europe do not, as we might expect, preserve the diffuse remnants of, say, Celtic or Norse or

Saxon mythology and religion. They seem to underpin all of these: in one sense, that of primal powers and images, they arose before these mythologies developed. In another sense, that of collective conserving and regenerating memory, they are the fusion of all myth, legends and religions of their lands, boiled down to a few potent verses. At the close of this chapter we will look briefly at the Vision of Thomas Rhymer, from oral tradition, involving one of those historical mortals who travelled to and from the faery realm. A more detailed analysis of the ballad is found in Appendix 3.

PAGAN RELIGIONS AND THE FAERY REALM

What relationship, if any, exists between the old religions and philosophies of the pagan world, and the faery and Underworld traditions? Initially we might expect to find many connections, and there is always the temptation to feel that in these traditions we have the 'pure' teachings of the druids, the bards, the great religions of the pre-Christian era. But the more we examine Norse or Celtic religion, the more we explore the heart of classical myth and legend, the more we find the elusive Underworld tradition as a vanishing constant. It is constant in the sense that it has always been acknowledged: the Romans and Greeks acknowledged its underpinning of their religions; the Celts based their entire world-view upon origins in the Underworld; Norse mythology has its potent Underworld powers and locations. But if we seek originals, definitive sources, it is ever receding, always about to vanish, yet still present.

Yet simple basics, such as the faery experience, always seem to be the property of an oral tradition. The more formalized a religious structure or order, the less likely it is to contain direct Underworld teachings. The Celtic druids and their heirs the bards, with their vast stores of cosmic and genealogical lore, their prophecies and visions, undoubtedly derived much of their energy from the Underworld, but were not an Underworld order in themselves.

Perhaps the key to this is the process by which religions become orthodox or politicized; the more formal, the more aligned to royalty, imperial policy and statesmanship, the further away from primal sources. The Underworld traditions are revolutionary: they cause static situations to revolve and change. Yet no formal religion has ever managed to obliterate Underworld traditions, or to remove the associated poems, tales, ballads and ritual practices from collective memory. This is perhaps why the essentially Underworld *Prophecies of Merlin*[14] survived as oral bardic poetry until the medieval period, when they were put into Latin by Geoffrey of Monmouth. They were not part of the orthodox religion, not even part of the formal bardic repertoire of genealogies and histories in Wales. They were the disturbing visionary products of the Underworld, and Geoffrey did not hesitate to use them to satirize and criticize contemporary politics.

If you wish to read some of the prophetic results of the Underworld initiation, the Prophecies of Merlin, and those of Thomas Rhymer in the thirteenth century are good examples.

DIRECT CONTACT

As faery contact is inseparable from the land, there are a number of simple techniques for making contact well-established in tradition. These involve typical faery locations which range from the great megalithic structures to very small unnoticed sites.

1. Faery bushes
2. Faery stones
3. Wild paths and earthworks
4. Springs
5. Certain fields
6. Trees (as distinct from bushes). Pair of trees as gate
7. The bottom land of gardens, fields, etc. Threshold places
8. Crossroads
9. Confluence points of streams and rivers

DISPOSING OF OR BREAKING FAERY AND UNDERWORLD CONTACTS

Just as there are many techniques for making faery contacts, there are others for breaking them. The most widely described is to use an iron blade, for faery beings do not like iron or steel. Many theories have been put forward for this belief, which is embodied in ceremonies involving the ritual cutting of faery contacts. Such ceremonies still seem effective today, and if you wish a dramatic and harsh separation from a faery companion, ritually cut a visualized line of contact with an iron or steel knife.

Historically inclined interpreters think that this aversion to steel comes from the fact that faery traditions are, essentially, Bronze Age. Religious interpreters use a rather clumsy piece of propaganda, suggesting that as steel is forged in a fire, and as faeries fear the fire of hell . . . (a version of this explanation is found in Robert Kirk). I personally prefer to think that there is some truth in the Bronze Age idea, but upon a deeper level. Many of the 'high' faery beings certainly appear in the guise of Bronze Age Celtic or pre-Celtic cultures, such as those described in early Irish epic and mythic poetry.[15] One of my earliest faery contacts involved some formal or ritualized greeting focusing upon a knife, and is worth recounting briefly here.

While visiting the woods near an ancient site in the early 1970s, I was startled by the sudden appearance of a short man in brown, soft leather clothing. He stood before me, holding out a long green stone or bronze leaf-shaped dagger, with many patterns upon the blade. He said, 'Brother, I have a good knife . . .' and waited for me to reply. I had no idea what to say, and after repeating the statement twice, he vanished. At the time I thought I had had some vision of a prehistoric native of the region, as I was close to one of the great stone circles of the Wessex culture. In retrospect I now think that this was a faery contact, with some kind of greeting formula, to which I should have known a response. The good knife was not of steel or iron.

I would guess that because the faery beings are non-technological, the forging of iron and steel represents our cultural breaking from them, our human separation from the holism of nature. I do not take any of this too literally and do not expect us to revert to a pre-iron age, but feel that on a very deep level this is the key to the traditional aversion of faery beings to steel or iron blades. Why this would not apply to bronze, I do not understand; most faery weapons or implements are of stone or bone, but bronze does not seem to be excluded.

Other, often inadvertent, breaks are caused by naming names or describing faery allies publicly. This last varies upon circumstances; it seems quite acceptable for people in group work in the faery and Underworld tradition to describe their contacts if they wish, among the group. But a public or flippant or boastful statement almost always results in severance. In some folk tales a spiteful or demanding faery contact is broken when the human discovers the faery being's name (such as in the famous tales of *Rumpelstiltskin* from Europe, or *Tom Tit Tot* from England).

FANTASY AND ROLE PLAYING

Because many of the traditions of the faery realm may seem to be connected to modern fantasy and role-playing games, films, books and similar entertainments, we need to be very clear in our definition and intent. The Underworld Mysteries are not, and never have been, anything to do with 'role playing' either in their ancient, collective traditional, or modern versions. The imagination is a powerful force if it is properly used, yet may dissipate energy through trivial entertainment just as easily as it generates through creative visualization.

Work within the faery realm is particularly prone to misunderstanding, and most people have no knowledge of the ancient enduring faery traditions, tending to compare these to modern fiction and fantasy as if the modern entertainments are the source and not a derivation. This misconception is corrected by practical work, in which the difference between empowered visualization with innerworld contact and role-playing or fantasy games is soon discovered.

In the development of visualizations, however, we need to be certain that no trace of fantasy entertainment is allowed, and that Underworld journeys do not become alternative computer games. There is always the temptation to fill in visualizations with preconceived dramatic visual sources, situations, entities and so forth. But traditionally this does not happen; only the simplest of traditional patterns, based upon the holism of the Three Worlds (Figure 1(b)) and the Seven Directions (Figure 3) are used, with detailed visions left free for interaction. There is a very different level of power in working with traditional archetypes or god and goddess forms, consciously contacted Underworld and faery beings, and fantasy entertainment with intentional heroic or magical themes. There is a good rule for developing visualizations that applies to any sequence or image or scenario: *if in doubt, leave it out.*

During a group weekend course on the Underworld tradition in England, a young woman said to me', But of course it's all fantasy, isn't it? I've never done visualization like this before, and I can feel the power of it . . . but it has no effect upon real life, does it?' In fact, the more we work with empowered visualization (setting aside, for the moment, work at sacred sites or natural power sites), the more effect the changes of energy and consciousness have upon our lives. With regular workings the energies will move outwards through our habitual patterns of life, and gradually change them. In some cases the changes are very dramatic and sudden, a typical Underworld catharsis. For most people the changes will really be felt after a full cycle of one year. But even one empowered visualization can change your life, for the Underworld and its realms are a source of incalculable power. Our own entities tap into this power by tuning in, by aligning our holism to the holism of the sacred land, the Underworld, the Light within the Earth.

This   is   the   essential   difference   between   modern   fantasy entertainment, in any presentation or form, and the power traditions. Both use imaginative structures, narratives, adventures, encounters. But the entertainment does not make deep permanent changes in our lives, it is merely entertainment. Some of this difference is a matter of intent, for empowered visualization requires intent and dedication. Some of it is to do with powerful collective consciousness, with images and themes that are inherent within our ancestral awareness, even if they are dormant or grotesquely commercialized today.

Conversing with the Ancestors

We find our ancestors in the Underworld. At least, it seems that way. It might be more accurate to say that when we enter the Underworld, we may enter into awareness of collective and individual ancestral memories and beings. One of the unusual features of ancestral contact in the Underworld is that it is at its strongest when the ancestors are remote in time: the further away they are in a linear chronology, the closer they are in contact with the Underworld. There is a considerable difference between ancestor lore in the perennial traditions (found worldwide) and the very modern occurrence of spiritualism and its loosely disguised New Age variant, channelling. The border line between ancestors, faery beings, and ancient gods and goddesses is often blurred, and it is with this blurring that we should begin our exploration of ancestral contact. Once we have clarified the overlapping areas, we may proceed with a few simple guidelines on ancestral contact within the Underworld.

Something occurs when we enter the Underworld which brings ancestral awareness alive within us. Folk tradition seems unconcerned with the blurring between ancestors and faery beings ... they dwell together in the faery realm, and this causes no problem. In relatively modern Gaelic tradition, for example, the mounds of churchyards were said to be temporary dwellings for the souls of the dead, and in time become faery hills. On a far larger scale we find the ancient origins of this belief concerning churchyards in traditions relating to the megalithic culture which flourished from at least as early as 5000 BC. the thousands of mounds, graves, artificial hills and chambers of the megalithic culture are widely understood to be faery dwellings.

This belief is less prevalent when it comes to stone circles and alignments, though these also have many faery traditions attached to them. In ancient Ireland we find that the gods and goddesses of the Tuatha De Danann, later known as the people of the Sidh, were given all the territory under the surface of the land after losing their war with the humans.[9] This tradition reflects a number of interconnected strands, both ancestral and faery. As the vast structures of the extended megalithic culture are unquestionably ancestral graves and dwellings, we would expect them to be mythic or imaginative focal points for ancestral lore and memories. But it is not sufficient to say that in time the memory of previous cultures becomes modified into a tradition of faery or Underworld beings ... for clear distinctions are frequently found, with repeated assertions that ancestors and faeries dwell together in the Underworld. The boundaries may indeed be blurred, but not through loss of memory or lack of understanding of the distinction between the two classes of being.

Ancient deities are also found within the Underworld and in the faery realm; these may be confused with ancestors through the long folk memory of pagan lore preserved through the ages. In faery tradition the gods and goddesses are often found in what might be loosely called *high* faery lore, which preserves pagan Celtic religion. There is a broad distinction between high and low faery lore. High faery lore is the body of tradition that talks of the ancient gods and goddesses of the land, usually the pagan Celtic deities. It also preserves tradition of kingship and ceremony, the Great Goddess, and the memories of the megalithic Bronze Age culture. Low faery lore is the commonly preserved lore found as late as the twentieth century concerning faeries, the faery realm, and the second sight. It includes faery companions, co-walkers, local traditions such as specific hills and mounds, faery nurses, faery lovers, and so forth.

High faery lore was preserved mainly in ancient texts and chronicles, and the long tales and ballads of the story-tellers. It increasingly passed out of oral tradition into literature by the twentieth century.

Low faery lore was preserved on an everyday level and remains active, in a diffuse and degenerate form, even today.

It should be remembered that many pagan deities are *not* found in the Underworld, as they belong on the surface of the land, or in the seas, rivers, sky, stars. There is no general rule that forgotten deities are relegated, so to speak, to a collective junkyard. Indeed, the concept of the Underworld as being synonymous with the unconscious mind, or the dustbin of collective beliefs, plays only a limited part in the Underworld tradition. We shall find in later stages of our exploration that there is a class of Underworld visions and dreams that seem to involve wandering through a storehouse of forgotten objects, piled at random. While we can give this a valid materialist psychological interpretation, it has deeper, more energetic connections to other aspects and realms of the Underworld that are not admitted in modern therapy.

WORKING OUTDOORS

Outdoor working falls into two general categories: those at ancient power sites such as temples, mounds, standing stones and so forth, and those at natural power locations. The second class includes natural rocks, springs, wells, confluences of streams, caves, trees. Methods of finding natural power locations are discussed on page 48.

Let us first look at a direct method of working at ancient power sites. Before going into techniques, it must be very clear that you undertake such work solely on your own responsibility, and that you are seeking to enter the Underworld of the site consciously and intentionally. Many people interfere with sacred sites in a trivial or 'experimental' way, and if the results are not to their liking they declare the *site* to be 'unhealthy' or 'weird'!

The Underworld tradition is attuned to the archetypal patterns that are inherent in the building of the ancient sites, and inherent in ancestral consciousness. Thus it provides a simple and powerful means of accessing sacred sites upon inner levels without resorting to open psychism, dowsing, or imposing any outside system of working upon the sites themselves. The entire basis is simple: the Seven Directions in Three Worlds (Figure 1b and 3).

Above, Below, Within, East, South, West, North

If you work with this directional attuning of consciousness and energy at any sacred site, you are aligning your own awareness to the collective awareness of humanity standing upon the planet, and to the general pattern of the sacred land and of power locations in the energy field of the planet. The Directions are natural, they are not a contrived system of interpretation. They hold inherent power. Work as follows:

1. A period of silence

2. Affirm the Directions with a simple formula such as:
   'The sky and stars above,
   The sacred land and Underworld below,
   The human and living spirit within.
   To the East is the power of Air, Dawn, Spring,
   To the South is the power of Fire, Noonday, Summer,
   To the West is the power of Water, Evening, Autumn,
   To the North is the power of Earth, Night, Winter.'

With this definition you are orientating the cycle of the seasons and elemental energies which is already inherent in the site, and which flows through it from day to day, month to month, year to year. This attuning assists and enables a fusion between your human awareness and the energies of the site itself. All other forces, such as the much-publicized energy vortices detected by dowsing, will flow unhindered within this holism. Working with such vortices is another separate discipline that may or may not be of use within the Underworld tradition.

3.   From the affirmation of the Directions, you calmly seek an entry into the Underworld at the site. If possible this should be at the centre of the site. The technique of visualizing a door or suitable entrance is effective, though you should be careful not to force imagery that is unsuited to the location.

   With practice it is possible to pass within and down into the Underworld of the site without the customary imagery, but use of the basic units such as door, tunnel, stair, and the corresponding return journey are strongly recommended until you have practised at a number of sites and are truly familiar with experiences of the Underworld and the beings and light within the Earth.

THE VISION AND JOURNEY OF THOMAS RHYMER

Of the small number of faery ballads preserved in oral tradition, two are particularly powerful and important as initiatory visions. The first is *Tam Lin* in which a girl redeems her lover from the Underworld and the Dark Queen; the second is *Thomas Rhymer* in which a journey through the faery realm is described. I have discussed both of these ballads in detail in *The Underworld Initiation* and other books,[16] and they are interconnected in a number of ways. A verse-by-verse analysis of the ballad of Thomas Rhymer is reproduced in Appendix 3.

   The vision of Thomas Rhymer is a major oral source of faery initiatory lore. As a ballad it was sung for centuries, and still exists in oral tradition in Scotland today. Thomas Rhymer or Thomas of Erceldoune (Earlston) lived in thirteenth-century Scotland. He was famous as a seer, with various vernacular prophecies attributed to him, the early prose *Tristan*, and a long Romance poem of his journey to Elfland or the faery realm. But the oral tradition preserved a simple stark ballad which, if we presume its origins to be thirteenth century, was preserved for 700 years by oral transmission. It may be that the vision itself is far older than its historical location, for the tradition can be traced back in various sources and legends of the Underworld or Otherworld, and the myth of the Sacred Apple and the Goddess.

The Ballad of Thomas Rhymer
Note: In this text some of the Scottish dialect words have been Angli-
cized for the general reader. Detailed texts in the Scottish vernacular are
found in F. J. Child's collection *The English and Scottish Ballads*.

1. True Thomas lay on a grassy bank,
And he beheld a lady gay,
A lady that was brisk and bold,
To come riding o'er the ferny brae.

2. Her skirt was of the grass-green silk,
Her mantle of the velvet fine,
And on every lock of her horse's mane,
Hung fifty silver bells and nine.

3. True Thomas he took off his hat,
And bowed low down to his knee,
'All hail thou virgin, Queen of Heaven,
For your like on Earth I ne'er did see'.

4. 'Oh no, oh no True Thomas' she said,
'That name does not belong to me;
I am but the Queen of Fair Elfland
That has come for to visit here with thee'

5. 'And you must go with me now, Thomas,
True Thomas you must go with me,
And you must serve me seven years,
Through good or ill as may chance to be'

6. She turned about her milk white steed
And took True Thomas up behind,
And aye whene'er the bridle rang,
The steed flew faster than the wind.

7. For forty days and forty nights
They wade through red blood to the knee,
And he saw neither sun nor moon,
But heard the roaring of the sea.

8. Oh they rode on and further on,
Until they came to a garden tree,
'Light down, light down, you lady fair,
And I'll pull of that fruit for thee'

9. 'Oh no, Oh no True Thomas' she says,
'That fruit may not be touched by thee,
For all the plagues that are in hell
Are upon the fruit of this country'

10. 'But I have bread here in my lap,
Likewise a bottle of red wine,
And before that we go further on,
We shall rest, and you may dine'.

11. When he had eaten and drunk his fill,
She said 'Lay your head down on my knee,
And before we climb yon high high hill,
I will show you wonders three.'

12. 'Oh do you see that broad broad road
That lies by the lily leven?
Oh that is the road of wickedness,
Though some call it the road to Heaven'

13. 'And do you see that narrow narrow road
All beset with thorns and briars?
Oh that is the way of righteousness,
Though after it few enquire.'

14. 'And do you see that bonny bonny road
Which winds about the ferny brae?
Oh that is the road to Fair Elfland,
And together there you and I will go'

15. 'But Thomas you must hold your tongue
Whatever you may hear or see . . .
For if one word you chance to speak,
You will never get back to your own country.'

16. And he has gotten a coat of woven cloth,
Likewise the shoes of velvet green,
And till seven years were past and gone,
True Thomas ne'er on earth was seen.

If we summarize the narrative we find the following stages:

1. Sleeping under a sacred tree, the hawthorn
2. Meeting the Faery Queen
3. Travelling with her into the Underworld
4. Wading through rivers of blood (sometimes of blood and tears)
5. Absence of Sun and Moon, but sound of roaring sea
6. Vision of garden and apple tree
7. Warning concerning the fruit
8. Fruit is transformed as bread and wine
9. Vision of three roads: Wickedness, Righteousness, Elfland
10. Service in Elfland, with gifts of green coat and shoes and the tongue that cannot lie
11. Return to human world

This vision is a classic source of how to conduct an Underworld experience, go there and back again. It also contains many of the power keys to the Underworld and faery initiations: the Dark Queen or Goddess, the land within the Earth, the sacred Apple Tree (conferring either madness or immortality), a ritual of transubstantiation, changing one deadly substance into another nourishing substance, the vision of three possible roads, and finally the gifts. The green coat and shoes are traditionally associated with the vitality of the land, while the tongue that cannot lie is the gift of truth-speech or prophecy.

This ballad preserves the way in and out of the faery realm, and the narration of the transformation and potential gifts to be found therein. A powerful training experience is to work with this ballad[17] and develop your own visualizations based upon its imagery and sequence. You may prefer to use some of the empowered visualizations in Part Two first, if you are not yet familiar with the Underworld and faery realm. The faery visualizations in this book use many of the elements defined in the traditional ballad of Thomas Rhymer, for these are the simple yet powerful basics of the faery tradition.

We can now move on to the technique of empowered visualization, and work with specific Underworld and faery exercises and visionary narratives.

In individual work, when you visualize and seek entry to the Underworld realms alone, you simply need to follow your own intuitions and not force any visions or encounters. Notes are helpful in this, for if you write out your impressions immediately after a working, they can be compared over a series of experiences and often give indications of the relative qualities or depth of perception. We tend to forget our altered states of consciousness quite rapidly, as the firm conditioning of our outer routine inevitably (and necessarily) reasserts itself.

In group work, particularly with members who have some experience of the Underworld and faery realm, it is usually possible to judge the depth of someone's experience, and assess whether the absence of formal images means a deeper contact or a protective limitation of perception. In very powerful sequences, group members frequently report 'blanking out' for certain parts of the narrative, and then quite naturally returning to a conscious perception of the developing sequence at a later stage. They pick up the further stages quite smoothly and naturally, without any feeling of loss of direction or confusion.

This apparent blanking does not diminish the experience, and usually indicates that there are depths of consciousness and energy at work which are not limited by form or a superficially temporal and linear sequence, such as the unfolding of the empowered narrative.

In working with the faery realm, or indeed any Underworld realm, we usually need specific means of entry and exit. The traditions provide many images and narratives and visions for this, but once you are within the Underworld there is no obligation to rigidly hold to every detail, and practical work shows that our consciousness often leaps into depths that are formless. People sometimes find this descent into formlessness confusing, and assume that it means that nothing is happening. In some ways it is the most powerful experience of all.

We also need to have a clear awareness of the rhythm between form, entity, and formlessness or energy. Our own forms, our bodies, are made of the energies of the land, of the Elements, of our spirit or ultimate Being. We have no firm form or appearance other than through the cycle of apparent time: our body dissolves and is regenerated every instant. The outer image of a person is not the inner reality; this is why human relationships are vast exploratory realms in themselves. Why should we demand any more rigid pattern in the Underworld, the world of rhythm and transformation between energy and form, the realm in which all death and life emerge out of one another?

Part 2

The exercises and visualizations are arranged in an unfolding or opening pattern of development. You will benefit most by working with them in this order, but the examples are not graded in the sense of 'beginner – advanced'; any exercise or visualization will work on both an advanced and an elementary level.

4. Empowered Visualization

As the term *empowered visualization* (my own term and definition) is used throughout this book, it is worth discussing what it means, and what happens during certain types of visualization. Although visualizing is an increasingly popular and widespread technique today, it can work upon various levels of consciousness, with a variety of effects.

Empowered visualization is something very specific; it involves a range of images and works through underlying patterns within the connecting sequence of the images. While sets of images or single images are relatively static, even when they are potentially powerful, it is often the pattern or combination of images that brings a response from within ourselves, and generates inner changes associated with such response. The art of defining and selecting these changes, through intent and rhythmic repetition, was well established in pre-materialist cultures. It can be restated for today.

In empowered visualization there are also embedded patterns and underlying shapes that are not immediately apparent; they may transcend or underpin, for example, a narrative such as those used in the older traditions.

A rambling tale with Otherworldly or Underworld imagery and characters can often be clarified if we are aware of the ground-plan, so to speak, upon which its standard patterns are laid out. Much of the interpretation of myth and legend seeks to place tales and themes upon or within such ground-plans. Modern interpretations frequently miss the basic patterns inherent in myth, legend and folklore. They do so by forcing the material into a psychological, sociological or materialist mould that simply did not exist in human life, in human consciousness, when the myths were part of daily experience. Curiously, if we find the right key or ground-plan to the mythic traditions, we can bring the inner force alive for contemporary use, even though we are far removed culturally from their sources.[18]

A typical simple, modern example of this would be a narrative involving the Four Seasons or Four Directions. Overt imagery might include four doors onto landscapes for each season and direction. Due to the holism of elemental patterns, many other potential and actual energies may be at work that are not shown in the basic imagery used for visualization through the four doors. (This pattern is used as the basis for the empowered visualization beginning on page 85, which works with the Four Directions as Underworld locations.) Our Figures 1 (page 10) and 3 (page 42) show some of the basic attributes of the Powers of the Directions or Wheel of Life.

Basic visualization works with the effect of holding specific images in the forefront of consciousness. Our imagination is our power-house; out of it, all energies and forms are generated. If the imagery and the visualization are only on the surface of consciousness, they may have no lasting effect. But certain images tap into the deeper levels of imaginative force within us; when these are combined within archetypal patterns they may have a permanent transformative effect.

The perennial wisdom traditions, ranging from orthodox religion to practical magic, all use this technique of combining specific images in patterns. As a rule the most powerful visualizations are those attuning to a lasting tradition. The tradition, whatever it may be, is itself attuned to, or sculpted out of, a collective stream of images. The collective imagery is usually environmental or cultural (see Figure 4).

It is this last level that we work with in the Underworld tradition and the faery contacts, for these are preserved for centuries within, and are regenerated out of, collective consciousness. Within this collective field, there are still specific techniques and images to be recovered, which in themselves revive and reawaken precise Underworld energies and experiences.

This is the polar opposite/partner of orthodox religious imagery, which seeks to subsume or absorb all collective traditions and modes of consciousness within its dogmatic or authoritarian structure. Underworld traditions pass directly to the collective levels, without attempting to convert or dogmatize them, and after that several perennial techniques and contacts crystallize out. We will be working with some of the more unusual levels of the Underworld tradition in *Power Within the Land*.

WHAT HAPPENS IN EMPOWERED VISUALIZATION?

The visions act as a medium for energy: they give form to forces inherent within both ourselves and the environment. There is no

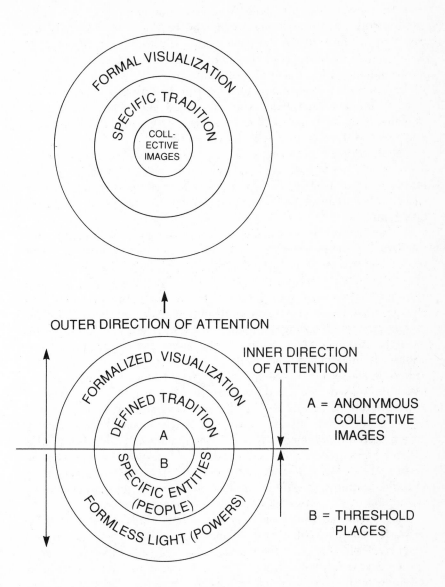

Figure 4 Consciousness and Tradition

suggestion, when we work with a complex visualization, that the images within it are 'real', but neither are they 'unreal'. By environment, we mean a total environment ... the holism of space, energy or consciousness, and relative time. It may be a purely local concern with a local energy or consciousness, or it may be the environment of our Lunar, Solar, or Stellar realms, the Three Worlds of ancient tradition. Empowered visualization crosses all boundaries, dissolves all filters and sets of limitations, if it is used properly.

Empowered visualization is distinct from free association or random fantasy, or even from intellectually predefined and guided visualization. It depends upon its patterns and images being in contact with deep energies and upon contact with actual entities.

The development of images in a sequence, held in the imagination of a group, is, initially, an amplified version of what happens in poetry, story-telling or theatre. The emphasis is always upon group involvement rather than passive reception, such as occurs in television entertainment.

It is not necessary for the images to be accurate or real, merely that they connect various levels or states of consciousness and energy. This is a subject that is frequently confused, and regularly misrepresented or abused in publication and practice. It is really a matter of intent and tuning: providing we stay with a coherent set of images, they will always work. There are no pure or definitive images, for form dissolves as our perception changes, tending towards energy in increasingly metaphysical shapes or presences. The entire matter of vision, consciousness, imagination, and form or entity is relative.

Certain shapes seem inherent at the deepest levels of consciousness; these are known through the glyphs or mandalas of world religion, power traditions, magic and mysticism. When outer awareness and regular thought patterns are stilled, when deeper levels of consciousness are accessed through meditation and contemplation, these patterns arise without bidding, appearing as images to the responsive inner vision. Conversely, outward models, maps, meditational symbols, sacred dance and other patterns, reveal the inherent glyphs or archetypical shapes to us, helping us to reattune our thought and energy patterns.

These glyphs are the primal or archetypal patterns within which more outwardly complex entities take shape, and through which they reiterate or run their relative cycle of energy. One reason for their occurrence in the consciousness of all people and cultures is that they are a deep reflection of the patterns of movement made by the planet, the Moon, Sun, and Stars. The Wheel of Life, for example, runs the cycle of the Four Seasons, Four Elements, Four Ages. But it also unites and defines the

Four (planetary) Directions of North, South, East and West with the seven inherent directions of Before, Behind, Right, Left, Above, Below and Within.

More simply, the universal power glyphs or mandalas are inherent within *physical* relationships, humanity upon the planet in the solar system, just as much as they are in consciousness. The esoteric traditions teach that there is no separation between the inner and outer patterns, the macrocosm and microcosm. In empowered visualization, we take sets of complex entities and energies (people, places, powers) and work backwards, so to speak, to use them to reach deep transformative patterns of power. This idea of universal pattern making, with increasingly and progressively complex entities coming out of simple energy patterns, is found in all traditions worldwide.

The secret, however, is to be consistent. Hopping from one set of images to another, from one tradition to another, dissipates our power. There is a curious result arising from working steadfastly within one spiritual or magical tradition for several years, and never deviating from it. Such constant intent and regular attuning will eventually enable you to work in any tradition, finding the inner connections beyond outer forms. But this is not possible without empowerment through traditional visions and techniques; it is not a matter of intellectual comparison or grand statements of 'all-is-oneness'.

A collective tradition has enormous power; the faery realm has been contacted and worked within by thousands and thousands of people over many centuries. This collective imaginative store of images, patterns, entities, forms and beliefs is a great powerhouse that we may tap into. Indeed, it is inherent within us, attuning to the Underworld and faery traditions of our land and of our ethnic inheritance, wherever and whoever we may be.

So when we work with empowered visualization in the faery realm what is happening? There are two valid ways of attempting to answer this question, if an answer is needed.

The first is the traditional understanding that we are actually working with faery beings who take on form according to specific images shared between our race and theirs. A common alphabet, in other words, not too distant from our own shapes and outer patterns. The faery and human races tend to look similar, to be close reflections of one another. The faery halls are real places, to which we may go in story, song, vision, or through physical translation.

Simply move with the collective knowledge and images, and the experience gradually becomes empowered, taking on a distinct quality and energy of its own, far beyond that of simple fantasy. The old traditions were taken literally and they work in a literal manner, giving back experiences and forms out of their common stock of images and potentials.

The second is upon a deeper level, known and taught in the initiatory arts, and possibly more acceptable to the modern mind. It is that the apparent shapes and experiences are presentations; they are mediums or interfaces between our outer consciousness and deeper levels of energy and perception. This should not be confused with a psychological interpretation that assumes that all experiences are the products of the psyche. There are real entities, real energies and real locations in the faery and Underworld experiences. They may not, however, be exclusively limited to the forms given them in collective tradition, even when these forms are at work and actively regenerate within our own imaginations.

Empowered visualization puts us in touch with specific people, powers, and places. These three pivots of any Mystery, *People, Powers, and Places*, may be found in innumerable dimensions, human and non-human, physical, non-physical, and metaphysical. The empowerment comes from the tradition itself, from the imagery, and from the intentional tuning or energy patterns of whoever guides or constructs the visionary sequence.

Nothing, after all, is exactly what it seems. The Gaelic seers taught that all beings interpenetrated one another, and that there was no living creature that did not have other living creatures upon or within it, even to the smallest invisible entity.[19] Modern science and biology have proved this teaching in a materialist sense, but upon imaging levels it still holds good.

The holism of living entities and energies is given variable patterns in our imagination: in visualization we intentionally change the patterns, replacing those of custom and habit with those of deeper and often cathartic power. So when we work with empowered visualization to enter the Underworld and faery realm, we are using the images to give form to energies and entities that we do not usually perceive. Despite our customary ignorance or exclusion of these people, places and powers, they are as real as we are. Which is to say that like ourselves, they have relative reality depending upon images and a cycle of energies.

SOME BASIC EXERCISES

There is a variety of what might be called full-scale visualizations and energy-aligning techniques that enhance our awareness of the Underworld. These elaborate narratives, originally preserved in oral tradition and, in the ancient cultures, temple training, also bring us into direct interaction with Underworld energies and entities. Both the traditional and modern forms, such as those in this book prepared from my own individual experience and from group work, bring transformation within ourselves, and eventually enable mediation of the Light within the Earth.

Our role as humans is, or ought to be, as mediators, as bridges between the worlds, bringing certain modes of consciousness and energy to other life forms that are separated to a greater or lesser degree. At present it seems that most of the separation is our own; we have cut ourselves off from all other forms of life and consciousness, including our own planet and our fellow beings upon it and within it.

Some examples and descriptions of the full-scale techniques form the main visualizations which follow, but there are also basic direct exercises which will repay regular work. These are very simple exercises in many ways, yet they are also the most advanced Underworld techniques, bypassing detailed visualization and working directly with energy itself.

I would recommend finding a balance between the visualized ima-ginative techniques, such as the narrative journeys (part of a venerable collective tradition), and the direct energy techniques, such as those which follow shortly. For most people, it is creative and repeated work with imagery, narratives, visualization, that awakens and realigns the energies. Other methods are ritual pattern-making, movement, silent meditation, and sink-or-swim encounter techniques, which are often found in primal or chthonic magic. After this awakening has occurred, and this is the *initiation*, the more direct techniques can be used at will.

The potent force of the imagination frees up our energy patterns and, if we use traditional initiatory techniques, gives us a framework of images that holds great potential for inner transformation. The same potent force can be used to degrade and enervate ourselves . . . as an isolated materialist might say unwittingly, *it is all in the imagination.*

We literally image what we are. Through rampant greed, indifference and materialism we have imaged ourselves into increasing antagonistic isolation; we reject all other orders of life, abuse them, deny their very existence. Then we wonder why humanity feels alone in the universe, why we turn upon one another in misery, rage and anguish. If we use our imagination to open ourselves out of our isolation, we find that the world is full of many beings, many realities. The *world* is not simply our planet, but the total environment, the universal world. In and of this universal world is our very substance, matter, the body. It is both our body, renewed daily out of the substance of the land, and the planetary body, with its different zones, continents, lands, and power places.

If we work with the Light within the Earth, the energy inherent in the Underworld within and beneath our conscious interpretation of our environment, remarkable changes occur.

Let us look at some simple exercises that enhance this interaction with the Underworld and its energies. In these exercises we are concentrating primarily upon energies rather than entities . . . the visualizations and traditional imagery give form to the beings, just as our own beings are given form through the collective image of humanity upon the land. These exercises have been developed in my own work over a period of fifteen years or more and I have designed them for general use by modern individuals and groups. There is another related set of older techniques embodied within various traditions which have the same effect, but are often confusing or inaccessible to the modern mind.

The Rising Light Below

This is a simple but major technique for arousing energy and passing it through your body: the power that rises from the Underworld, the light within the Earth, will awaken and transform your own energies far more effectively than concentrating in isolation upon your power centres or *chakras*. If you do this exercise once every day, and also work with visualization techniques on a regular basis, you will realign and activate your own energy centres rapidly.

This exercise is the mirror-working to those well-publicized techniques which call down light 'from above'. In both cases the energy seems to begin outside the individual (though this understanding changes as you develop your inner powers), but in this technique the light is inherent within the Underworld, often in a latent mode. Human awareness activates the power, and draws it up through the body of the land into the human body. The Rising Light Below exercise is most effective while standing, though it may also be done sitting cross-legged, as squatting and cross-legged postures all enhance our earth contact. Here are the stages, with some brief notes on their development and effect:

1. *Begin with a period of silence and steady regular breathing.* Your arms are lowered, with the fingertips stretched and pointing towards the ground. If you are sitting they may touch the ground lightly or rest upon your thighs. This initial arm position is important, as you will be raising your arms to different positions through the exercise.

2. *Be aware of the point of contact between your body and the ground.* If this is

the floor of a room be aware that the building is in contact with the ground, with the land. For obvious reasons this type of exercise is enhanced by working directly upon the surface of the land, or in a cave, basement or underground chamber. By the holism, paradox, or 'law' of reflections and octaves, it also works very well in high places, such as the tops of hills and in tall buildings. Many Underworld techniques are useful for those of us who live in a city environment, as they pass directly through the imbalanced enervating city energy field, which has little or no effect upon them. If you live in an unhealthy, energy-isolated building, do this exercise on the roof or in the basement as well as in your own apartment.

3.   *Visualize a source of energy just below the ground or floor where your feet or body make contact.* This is usually felt and seen as a glowing ball of light. The upper surface of this energy sphere touches the soles of your feet (or your legs, thighs and buttocks if you are sitting in a cross-legged position), and from its lower surface a strand of light descends into the heart of the land, into the depths of the planet to an unknown source. This is your reflected energy field in the Underworld, normally latent. You are going to activate it, bring it alive through conscious work. Remember that it is part of you, reflected energy which you do not normally access or use, something of which millions of people are completely unaware, even those who practise meditation and energy techniques.

4.   *Increase your awareness of this energy sphere*: feel it touching you, move your imagination into it. You may feel your personal energies descending into it, and a sensation of heat where your body touches the ground.

5.   *Gradually draw the energy source into yourself.* This is done by breathing steadily and feeling the energy sphere rise through your feet into your body. Your arm/hand position is slowly raised, drawing the energy with it. There are four zones of the body/energy field: FEET/GENITALS/HEART/THROAT (HEAD) (see Figure 5). These are our human reflections of the holism of the Elements and Worlds (see Figures 2 and 3, pages 34 and 42).

6.   *FEET: be aware of the Element of Earth,* and the matter or substance of your entire body. The energy sphere rises up through your feet, legs and thighs. This is the first awakening of energy within your physical substance. Your arms are still directed downwards, but slowly raised, drawing the energy as they move.

7.   *GENITALS: be aware of the Element of Water,* and the twofold nature of water in your body. Firstly it is the fundamental element of your cells; on a non-physical level Water is the element of creation, birth, sexual union, love, and represents the second awakening of energy within your physical substance. Your arms are raised gradually to waist height.

8.   *HEART: be aware of the Element of Fire.* As the energy sphere rises, it gradually becomes more incandescent. The Four Elements are simultaneously literal and metaphysical. At this heart level, the increasing

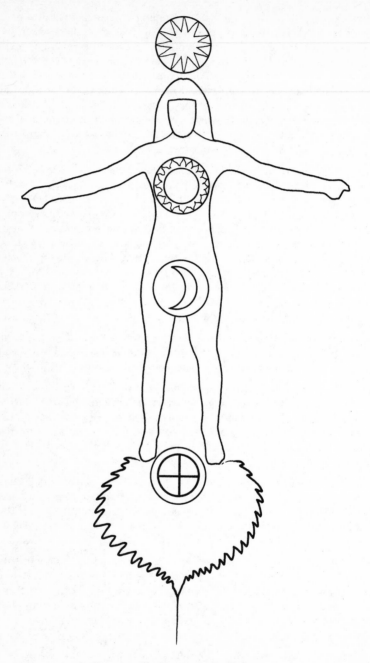

Figure 5 The Rising Light Below

rate of your energy becomes fire. In your body this is bioelectrical energy, the flow of blood, and the subtle forces that radiate from your life core. As these subtle forces manifest they appear in an increasingly watery and earthy form. The incandescence of the energy sphere rising from the Underworld through your body is the third awakening of energy within your physical substance. Your arms are raised, palms upwards, to shoulder height.

9.   *THROAT (Head): be aware of the Element of Air.* The energy has now risen to surround your head and shoulders (see Figure 5), and has reached its most rapid and mobile rate. All four zones are now alive, each rising level through the body being merged one within another. Yet the elevation of energy towards the head causes an increase in rate, and changes of your consciousness. Your arms are raised above the head, palms upwards.

10.   *Returning the power.* Simply reverse the sequence by steadily lowering your arms, and feeling the power pass down through your body. It returns steadily to your energy sphere within the land, below your feet. As it descends, you lower your arms, and each of the four zones gently reduces in activity.

Meditation Within This Technique

As this is an energy arousal technique, you need not pause and meditate within it at all. Meditation, however, will greatly enhance the effect, and will put you into conscious awareness of the energies in and through your body. Pausing for meditation works best after you have developed the raising and lowering technique in its own right. In other words, do not use this exercise and begin to meditate upon each of the four zones in depth until you have completed the full cycle several times.

You may meditate upon each zone as it rises, or as it descends. As this involves arm movement, remember that you will feel tension in your arms and body. These tensions were used in ancient temple training as sources of power, and the arm positions have a strong effect upon the flow of energy through your body.

AN ESSENTIAL NOTE.   When you raise the energy sphere to the Throat/Head zone, hold it there. This is the most ecstatic zone in terms of meditation, and there is often a tendency to lose some of the simple control. Your arm position and tension serve to keep the energy field in the head zone. You should not attempt any imagery or action by which the energy sphere rises away above your head and disperses. Remember you are drawing up the subtle force of the Underworld, and of your own being reflected in that realm, and not making an offering or seeking to share or disperse your energy as you might in religious devotion or sexual ecstasy.

You may feel an ecstatic sense of union, have visions of stars and, most of all, a response from the light above which is the consciousness of our Sun as a spiritual being. If you do experience this (and though many people do, not everybody does), do not rush off into it, as you will simply lose your energy. Always aim to pass the power back through your body: anything that is harmonized from the Direction of Above will flow with your intent, and pass through you into the land.

So little conscious work is done today with the land and the Underworld realms that circulating energy in this way is an essential work of sharing, transformation and affirmation of the spirit inherent in matter.

When your energy sphere is returned to the latent position, reflecting just below the ground, you will find that your awareness of the land, the natural world and many subtle energies and beings is enhanced. Finally, as always, make some brief notes.

The next stage of this energy working is to pass energy in and out of specific locations, objects and other life forms, such as plants and trees. We will work specifically with this method of passing energy in *Power Within the Land*, but many aspects of it are scattered through the present book.

A Basic Underworld Visualization

The major visualizations used in this book are designed to establish specific contacts and generate broadly defined experiences within the Underworld and faery realm. Many areas are left intentionally open, but the overall framework comes from tradition, reworked for modern use. If we reduce the basis of such empowered visualization to a very simple sequence, we have a pattern which may be worked in its own right, or into which specific images or intentions may be woven.

1. A period of silence

2. Affirming the Four Directions

3. Visualizing a circular closed door or hatchway in the floor before you. If the working is done with a group, they sit in a circle and collectively visualize the closed doorway in the centre.

4. Open the door, with a clear affirmation of your intent to enter the Underworld and seek the Light within the Earth. If you wish to reach a particular location, zone or specific contact, define this now.

5.   See a steeply descending spiral stair, curving to the right. This stair is cut out of natural rock. Along the wall on the left-hand side is a thick rope woven of red, black and white strands, fixed into the rock by stone or bronze fastenings. Descend the stair.

6.   The stair descends into a cave, chamber or hollow within the Earth. Sometimes this is a simple underground temple. Usually you pass through an archway under which a small lamp hangs, shedding a faint guiding light. In the chamber beyond the archway, you pause in silent contemplation. At this stage various contacts may be made or visions experienced.

7.   Return through the archway and ascend the stairs.

8.   Climb out through the circular doorway and close it behind you. See the doorway fade into the floor of the room in which you began your visualization.

9.   Discuss if necessary, and take notes.

Notes

If you intend to work regularly with the Underworld tradition, you will find that simple note-taking can be helpful, but it need not be lengthy or obsessive. The most valuable things to note immediately on finishing a visualization, either in private or at an outdoor site, are likely to be the following:

1.   Any symbols upon the door or over the archway.

2.   Describe the cave, chamber or underground temple. It is usual to begin with a very simple rock chamber, but this often changes aspect into a related location. These spontaneous changes of location are important, and you may return to such a place at will. The initial notes will help you to remember details for future visualizations, and for correlating dream work.

3.   Describe any people, beings or objects that appear within the cave or temple during your meditation. Objects that you are offered as gifts are particularly significant, as these are often keys to further working and may be used in separate meditations upon their power and meaning, or as gifts that you tender at later stages of your work.

4.   Describe the energies or power that you experience while in the Underworld, and how these affect you when you emerge from the working.

Dreams

After empowered visualization at power locations or in private work-ings, you may have unusual dreams. Any such dreams should be noted down, and compared with the effects of your visualizations. Once again it is not necessary to keep a bulky record or detailed notes, merely to be aware of any dreams that you have involving Underworld images and powers, and to compare these to your waking visualizations and visions.

We can now begin to open out and expand upon the two basic modes (energy work and visualization) in more detail.

5. The Dark Goddess and the Tree Below

After a period of silent meditation, Sacred Space is defined and enlivened.*

Our intention is to seek the primal Underworld Temple and enter the presence of the Dark Goddess. To approach this reality within the Earth, we must build the way within our creative vision, giving imaginative form to the energies at work.

First we see in the floor, in the centre of the circle, a circular wooden door. As we look upon this door, we see a sign or symbol cut into its dark wood.

Now the door opens in two equal halves, revealing a passageway below. We walk towards the opening, and see a steep flight of spiralling stairs, turning always to the right. These are of rough stone, cut directly out of living rock. Along the left-hand wall we see a thick braided rope, made of three strands coloured red, black and white; it is fastened to the wall by bronze pins, each one having the head of a dragon holding the rope in its jaws.

One by one we enter the steep stairway and begin to descend, holding the triple rope for balance. The descent is steep, and there is only a faint light from far below. Soon we have left the upper world behind, and as we

---

*Sacred Space is defined by briefly visualizing and relating to each of the directions in turn (see Figure 3). This preliminary attuning of awareness greatly enhances any inner work which follows.

In group work the narrative may be read aloud by one member, or taken from a prerecorded tape.[10] For individual work you can use a tape, but the simple method of reading the narrative *aloud* to yourself is surprisingly effective. After several practice sessions you will be able to work with the vision without extensive reading aloud. The key to this is in the perennial power of story-telling . . . a story or vision shared between the imagination and the voice is highly empowered. It works with your own voice just as effectively as with someone else's.

descend we feel the presence of the rock all around us. There are faint vibrations in the stone from time to time, as if a deep resonance passes through the fabric of the Earth. As we descend we feel a growing warmth, which seems to come from all round, yet the walls of the rock stairway are cool to touch. We feel the presence of the inner fire, and respond to it. [*Short pause here.*]

Now we reach the foot of the stairs: there is a low opening and over it hangs a tiny lamp, glowing with a steady white flame. One by one we affirm our intention to pass through into the Temple of the Underworld and meet the Dark Goddess, if she chooses to be present.

We emerge into a dark cavern, with only the faintest of light reflected from the tiny lamp, barely enough to see by. In the centre of the cavern is a still, black pool of water. One by one we step forward and look into the pool. At first we see reflections of our faces, dim and obscure, then the image changes, and we look upon whatever is revealed to us in the pool of the Underworld. [*Pause for contemplation and vision here.*]

Gradually we come out of the visions in the pool, and as we do so we become aware that someone is present on the other side of the water. In the dim light, we look across the pool, and see there a flight of steps leading up into a dark cleft in the rock. Standing at the top of the steps is the figure of a woman, in a black robe and deep hood. We cannot see her face. In one hand she holds a distaff, from which a thread falls to a spinning spindle. As the spindle turns it flashes brief instants of colour, as if it reflects the light of the lamp over the entrance by which we came into the temple. If we seek to approach the Dark Goddess, we must walk around the pool and approach the opposite shore.

One by one we pass around the pool, walking to the left, and turning sunwise to reach the flight of steps. Suddenly the dark figure stands before us at the foot of the stone stairs. One by one we approach her, and are bidden to offer that which we most wish to keep. This must be a true offering, and no deceit is possible.

We offer our gifts to the Dark Goddess, the lady of perpetual change and regeneration, who both conceals and reveals the light within darkness. We commune with her in silence. [*Pause for contemplation here.*]

Now we emerge from our communion, and find that our offerings have been exchanged for something in return. As this realization comes to us, a faint glowing light begins to emerge from the cavern walls. At first it is a rose colour, then it becomes yellow and green, and finally it blossoms into a brilliant white. The black pool becomes a silver mirror of light, and the cavern is radiant. We see images carved upon the walls, telling a story that we remember. [*Silent pause here.*]

When we look again for the figure of the Dark Goddess, we find that she has disappeared. Above, in the rocky wall of the cave, is a dark cleft at the top of the flight of stairs. Despite the brilliant light it remains in shadow. Now a choice is given to each of us: we may remain and contemplate the

Light within the Earth, or we may try to approach more closely to the Goddess by ascending the flight of stairs towards the cleft in the rock. Make your choice, and be at One. [*Silent pause here.*]

Now we are bidden to return to the outer world. One by one we return to the shore of the pool, and in the light of the cavern see the shape of two serpentine interwoven creatures in the depths, ceaselessly coiling and moving to and fro, making patterns that radiate power up through the waters and into the cavern. We feel this power flow through us, rising through the soles of our feet and passing up to our genitals, and our hearts, our throats, our heads. When the power flows through our entire bodies, it is time to leave the Underworld Temple.

We walk round the pool towards the entrance on the opposite side, and as we do so the light of the Temple dims gradually. When we reach the low entrance with its tiny lamp burning overhead, the cave is in darkness. Yet we feel the resonant power of the Underworld flowing through us, as if we are filled with fire and light. This is the power that we will carry back to the upper world, and bring out to sanctify the land.

One by one we climb the long steep flight of stone stairs, feeling the faint resonance of the rock pulse through us. Now we reach the doorway to the upper world, and climb through it. We emerge into a dim, grey room, seeming shadowy and vague. Gradually it realigns as the outer world, and we return to our position in the circle, where each of us began the journey. We see the door close, the equal halves of its dark wooden circle folding shut.

Now the door fades, leaving only the floor of the room. We open our eyes, and return to outer awareness.

Now we move on to the first empowered faery visualization. Although there is no sense of progression from beginner to advanced in these exercises, they are mutually enfolded or interlaced. The sequence in which they appear is a powerful working pattern in itself.

The Tree Below

Sacred Space is dedicated and opened. If working in a group, members should sit in a circle. If two people are working, they sit opposite one another; if three, in a triangular relationship; if four, in a square. The aim is always to visualize into the centre of a circle.

In the centre of the room we see a well in the floor. Build this image strongly: a circular well in the centre of the room, with a shallow rim. Now it becomes substantial as we look upon it, and we see that many fine roots are gripping the edge of the well, mingled deep into its fabric. These roots hold a fascination for us, and we long to look closely at them.

We rise and gather around the well, and one by one lean over and look within. The fine roots lead away into the depths below, lit by a blue-green light. We see that as they stretch away from us the roots thicken, leading into an indistinct brown shape that seems to float upon blue-green light below. At first the sight is blurred, as if something floats half-submerged in hazy waters.

Suddenly the image clarifies, and we realize that we are looking upon a tree. This tree is of such immense size that we could not register its image at first; it grows in reverse within the well, its roots around and within the rim, its crown far below. We follow the shape of the roots, leading our sight to a long brown and green trunk, leading deeper still to a huge spread of branches and leaves, far, far below. The blue-green light is reflected up through the leaves from an unseen source in the depths. We look for some time upon this inverted tree, with its roots in our world and its crown far below in the light. [*Brief pause here for meditation.*]

This is one of the trees of transformation, an inverted tree leading to another world. We know that if we wish to reach that world, we must climb the tree, from its roots to its crown, ever downwards. One by one we affirm our intent to travel the tree, and climb over the edge of the well.

At first the way is difficult but as we progress, it becomes easier, with the widening roots supporting us as we descend. When we reach the wide platform where the roots emerge from the trunk, we pause and look below. The broad tree trunk stretches away beneath us, with immense branches growing out of it at intervals. This is the way that we must travel to the realm below. We see the branches spread out into an immense crown with shimmering silver and green leaves in constant motion, and below that a green blur of light that confuses our sight when we try to focus upon it.

Now we climb onto the trunk, and find that deep folds and grooves in the bark make movement possible, giving foot and hand holds before we reach the first great branches. One by one we climb onto the trunk, and feel the massive strength of the tree support us in our descent. Now we look up, and see for the first time that above us is a curious sky. It seethes with purple, blue and silver colours, with lines of light moving to and fro across it. Directly above our heads as we look up is a circular hole in the sky, with the roots of the tree disappearing into it. This hole is muddy brown and black, as if the roots penetrate into a circular bed of earth above.

Now we descend the trunk, and find that the way is increasingly easy. As we reach the great branches, a feeling of balance and lightness flows through us, as if we have left superfluous weight behind. Now we can see beyond the crown of branches, and realize that the green blur is a flat grassy plain far below. As we climb down, the branches and leaves gradually hide this plain from us, until we see nothing but the tree around us. Deeper into the crown, we feel a crisp cool wind blowing around us, invigorating and exciting.

Now we are upon the slimmest branches, amid a vast cloud of rustling,

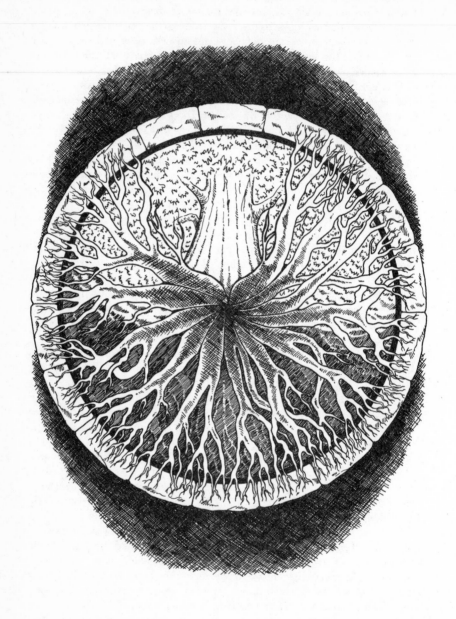

seething leaves glittering in the brilliant light. Suddenly we realize that the grassy plain is only a short jump away, and one by one we let go of the branches. We fall lightly to the ground, and as our feet touch it we feel a thrill, a current of power flows through us for the briefest instant. We stand at the point where the branches of the tree barely touch the land below, and for a moment look up at the great crown and trunk leading far into the sky above, vanishing into a black hole. The sky has changed colour, and becomes blue and silver, emitting a sourceless light that illuminates the land brightly.

Now we turn and look across the plain. It stretches away, flat and green in all directions. The grass is full of tiny brilliant flowers and constantly waves to and fro, sometimes with the direction of the wind, sometimes against it. We turn into the cool wind and look out across the featureless plain. The steady flow of air makes our eyes water, and we turn our backs to the wind and look in the opposite direction. Far across the plain we see a mound. It seems to be a low grassy mound, with no distinguishing features.

We know that we must walk towards this mound, and one by one set out with the wind at our backs.

As we move towards the mound our progress is fast; we find that we speed across the ground as if helped by the wind at our backs and the grassy earth beneath our feet. We are filled with deep power, as if every life energy within us is clarified, amplified, aroused. As we approach the mound we see that it is a huge grassy hill, long, smooth and featureless as if worn by wind and rain for thousands of years.

Now we reach the foot of the mound and look up to its top. The grass and flowers flow over it without break or change, as if it has been folded up out of the plain without a break. Yet we know that we must enter into this mound, for our intent is to meet the People of the *Sidh*, the Faery Dwellers in the Mound. The summit seems to flicker with a faint light from time to time, invisible if we look directly at it, yet clearly seen out of the corner of our eyes. There are no paths, no markers, and no sign of an entrance in the smooth grass wall before us.

Our intent is now to walk round the mound and seek an entrance. We form this intent carefully, and one by one turn to the left and begin our walk, following the shape of the mound, traversing its length. As we walk the wind suddenly changes direction and blows into our faces. It seems to resist our passage, but we steadily walk forward until we reach a state of balance between our motion and the wind in our faces. As we reach the far end of the long mound, the wind suddenly drops. In the stillness we hear a faint sound, like distant music, seeming to come from the ground beneath our feet. [*Short pause here.*]

We make a turn to our right, around the side of the hill. Suddenly we come upon an entrance. It is a low stone box, made of two upright slabs roofed with a third massive capstone. It juts out of the turf before us, and we step round to look inside.

Within this small chamber we see someone sitting. This is the Doorkeeper of the Faery Mound, and for a few moments we look upon each other, beings from different worlds. [*Silent pause here. If the journey is led actively the door-keeper may be described.*]

The Doorkeeper signs that we should enter the chamber, which is very small. We have to bend, and immediately find that before us is a rough stone wall with no further access to the hill. We look upon this wall, and as we do so it begins to slide up into the earth above, revealing a glowing red light from within. There is a sense of urgency as it rises, and we quickly step through into the red glow beyond.

As we enter the mound the red light changes into a brilliant illumination of green, blue and white, and we find that we are standing upon a smooth stone floor inside the hill. Behind us the stone slab lowers, closing off the gateway. We are in the Faery Hall.

To our surprise, the chamber extends to our right and left, yet we entered by one end of the hill, and expected it to stretch away before us. We see a roof of natural stones tightly laid together and rising in a curve. Through these huge stones roots emerge, although there were no trees above the mound. The brilliant light comes from flaring torches in the roots, as if certain roots are alight. The stone floor of the chamber is marked with a complex interwoven pattern, rambling in all directions, seeming to elude sense, yet be full of meaning and direction.

First we look to our left, and see there assembled a host of faery beings. They are of many kinds and shapes, wearing costumes from many ages. Most are human in shape and dress, though many wear costumes of strange materials, while yet others are unlike any sort of being that we have seen before.

Now we look to our right, and see a great table at the far end of the hall. Behind this table are two tall thrones; one is made of rock and crystal, while the other is the huge stump of an ancient tree, still sprouting tiny branches and green shoots. Upon the rock throne sits the Faery Queen; upon the tree throne sits the Faery King.

We look first at the Queen. She has a white face and long flowing red and black hair. She wears a gown interlaced with veins of silver, gold and crystal, and we see faint patterns bloom and move upon her face. Now we look upon the King. He has curling hair and beard, shot through with golden streaks. He wears a simple green tunic with a pattern of white flowers upon it, and his arms are bare.

We approach the tables, and as we do so we see the King and Queen in more detail. As we draw near to the Queen the patterns upon her face seem to bloom and fade, like an interlacing of faint stems and leaves; her eyes are the fathomless eyes of a hawk. As we draw near to the King we see that his hair and beard seem woven with green wires or tendrils, and that his eyes are a deep green with black pupils. As we draw closer we see their eyes change colour suddenly when they focus upon us.

Upon the great rough table of stone there is food and drink, cups and vessels. We are drawn to either the King or the Queen, and one by one we approach whichever of the two draws us. Now we commune with the King or Queen in silence. [*Silent contemplation and visualization here.*]

We are aware that the King and the Queen have exchanged something with each of us, and that we are bidden to turn and view the faery hosts. Looking down the length of the great hall, with its burning root-torches and silver-green light, we realize that out of the crowd certain beings have stepped forward. We are invited to choose companions from among those that come forward to us.

Look closely upon those that offer themselves as companions. You may select one to be your partner, making a bond between the faery world and our own. You need not accept whoever comes to you first, nor do you need to choose any partner at all. But you may only pick a partner from among those that come to you freely, and not from those that hold back. If you choose a faery companion, do so carefully. If you do not choose a companion, be aware of your reasons for not choosing. [*Pause in silence here.*]

Now we have chosen companions, or decided to leave without companions. (*Note: Your companions can return with you and act as co-walkers or allies for future work between the human and faery realms.*) The size of our company has increased, and we know that it is time to leave the Faery Hall. We walk towards the entrance stone, and when we reach it hear the sound of wild music starting amid the faery host. We long to stay, but know that we must leave. By the entrance stone we see the figure of a woman, in a long robe and deep hood. She holds a basket of woven reeds on one arm, and from it takes a gift for each of us as we reach the door. We cannot see her face, but we look closely upon the gift that she has given, and keep it safe.

Now the door stone slides upwards and we step out into the tiny chamber beyond. There are three steps up to the door chamber, and as we go up, the light behind us seems to turn red, and we hear the sound of shrill pipes and mellow harps. The stone slab slides shut behind us, and we see that the Doorkeeper is beckoning to us to hurry through the chamber and out into the land beyond.

As we emerge we feel a strong wind blowing, with tiny drops of rain. It blows us back towards the tree. Looking in that direction we see only a spiralling column of smoke, faint and changeable, where the tree should be. There is a sense of urgency about our return to the tree, and we hear many creatures scurrying and running in the grass all around us, though we see nothing. We pass at great speed across the plain, and as we travel feel the quality of the light change.

As we draw near to the tree, it suddenly snaps into view, and we arrive suddenly at the point where its huge crown almost touches the grassy plain. The branches are whipped by the rising wind, and the leaves rustle and hiss loudly. From out of the heart of the leaves and branches two tall creatures step. They seem to be made of living branches, and each has a broad green leaf for a face. To each of us they come, one by one, and touch us upon the forehead.

With that touch we lose all sense of sound and for a moment experience the life of a tree or plant. We long to reach into the soil and up into the sky to the light, and experience a sense of time that is quite different from human time. [*Pause here.*]

Gradually we become aware again of the wind blowing hard upon us, and know that we must return to the human world. We climb up into the branches of the tree, and begin our long ascent. The two tree-creatures have disappeared, but as we climb we are aware that our faery companions and allies move with us, though we cannot see them. As we climb up the great tree trunk into the roots above, the land below blurs into a blue and green cloud, and we see above us a spiralling whirlpool of black and brown, into which the tree roots grow.

Now we approach that whirlpool, and it slowly ceases to spin, becoming a dark circular hole. On the other side of that hole there is a dim grey light, and one by one we climb through the well into a familiar room. At first it seems a shadow room in a grey dream, but we return to our original starting point, where we commenced our journey, and the room takes substance.

Now we look upon the well and the roots growing around it in the centre of the room, and it slowly fades, to be replaced by the solid floor. Our journey to the faery realm is over, and we return to outer consciousness, realizing that we have brought with us gifts and companions. [*Silent pause here.*]

(Notes are made and, if required in group work, people take turns to describe their experience. You do not have to describe your gifts or faery companions if you feel that you should not do so.)

6. The Four Cities

There are four cities that no mortal eye has seen but that the soul knows; these are Gorias, that is in the East; and Finias that is in the South; and Murias that is in the West; and Falias that is in the North. And the symbol of Falias is the stone of death, which is crowned with pale fire. And the symbol of Gorias is the dividing sword. And the symbol of Finias is a spear. And the symbol of Murias is a hollow that is filled with water and fading light.

The Little Book of the Great Enchantment   *Fiona Macleod*

Sacred Space, the Seven Directions, is a powerful key to working within the Underworld and the faery realm. The Directions and the Elements of Air, Fire, Water and Earth act as a relative pattern for our energies and consciousness when we explore other worlds and interact with their inhabitants. In working with the faery realm, the Four Directions of East, South, West and North carry a wealth of associations, particularly as the land is attuned to the energies of the Four Directions.

This directional pattern of energy, zoning and harmonizing the land, was a feature of ancient Celtic culture, and indeed of many cultures worldwide. It is still found inherent within our planetary directions today, and is not a theorized pattern but a practical one based upon the polarity of the Earth and the movement of the planet around the Sun.

The associations of the Seasons and Elements with the Directions is, therefore, a holism within which a relative cycle of energy occurs. We may use this cycle of the Directions and its seasonal and elemental energies in our visualization of the faery realm.

When we do so, we attune to the sacred land, with its empowered Directions, and simultaneously relate and attune the Elements and phases of consciousness (the Seasons) within ourselves. In many wisdom traditions involving transpersonal development, the Elements and related cycles, often called the Wheel of Life, form the basis of all

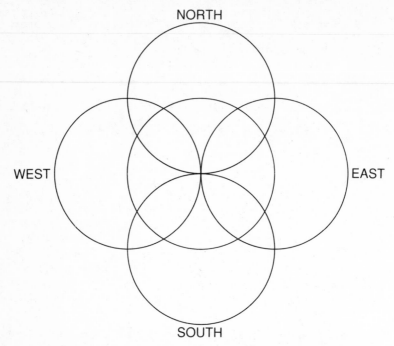

Figure 6 The Five Zones of Ancient Ireland. Many lands were modelled according to the Five Elements and Seven Directions in ancient cultures around the world.

meditation, visualization, and ritual pattern making. When this holism is realized within the faery realm, we find that it takes on characteristics of that realm, and also enables the powers of the land to be realized and manifested for us, within us, and so through us towards the regeneration of our own world.

> Wind comes from the spring star in the East; fire from the summer star in the South; water from the autumn star in the West; wisdom, silence, and death from the winter star in the North
>
> The Divine Adventure   Fiona Macleod

Fiona Macleod (William Sharp, 1855–1905) used an obscure model of four cities in several poems. These are said to be the original dwellings of the Tuatha De Danann, and are listed in early Irish poetry. The concept is closely related to the ancient provinces of Ireland (see Figure 6) and the Four Implements or magical weapons of the Tuatha De Danann, the ancient

Irish gods and goddesses who in later oral and written traditions became identified with the high faery race.[3]

The implements or Hallows are the Sword, Spear, Cup or Cauldron, and Stone. We may use this directional pattern and the four Otherworldly 'cities' in visualization, revealing the deeper mysteries of the faery realm. If we explore the four cities or convocations of the faery people, we enter the deepest levels of both faery and ancestral knowledge and energy, for they are at the foundation of mythic awareness of the relationship between human and faery realms.

The following visualizations should be done after working with the narrative vision of the Inverted Tree. They lead to deeper levels of the faery realm, and connect to powerful forces within the sacred land.

Note: Four meditational objects may be arranged upon a central small stand for these visualizations. They are (North) a quartz-veined stone; (West) a bowl of water; (South) a straight branch (pulled in one swift motion or cut without steel or iron from the tree); and (East) a dagger or small sword of bronze or stone (not iron or steel). A meditational glyph for this visualization is shown in Figure 7. With practice this pattern can be used directly in meditation to invoke the contact of the Four Cities and Four Powers.

The Four Cities

Sacred Space is opened, and silence is realized.

We begin by building strongly in our inner vision the Four Directions of North, East, South and West. In the North is night and winter; in the East is dawn and spring; in the South is noon and midsummer; in the West is autumn and evening.

As we build our vision of the Directions, we see the room in which we sit change into a square chamber, with a door in the wall of each Quarter, and know that we must pass through each door in turn to reach the Four Cities of the faery realm: Gorias in the East, Finias in the South, Murias in the West, and Falias in the North.

EAST: First the door in the eastern wall opens, revealing a landscape beyond. We look upon the gateway of the East: it is in the form of two standing stones, with a narrow gap between them. Through this gap we see a spring landscape, lit by pale blue and green light.

SOUTH: Next the door in the southern wall opens, revealing a landscape beyond. We look upon the gateway of the South: it is in the form of two trees, one of green spreading branches and the other a tree of flame, constantly burning but never consumed. As we look upon these trees, they

Figure 7 The Glyph of the Four Cities of Gorias, Finias, Murias and Falias. This glyph acts as a map for the empowered visualization (page 87–102) and also works as a meditative and visualizing key pattern or mandala. Patterns of this sort have a long association with faery and Underworld contact.

seem to exchange with one another; first one is of flame then of green branches, then the other. We look between them and see a brilliantly lit land, with a distant hill rising directly in the centre of our line of sight.

WEST: Now the door in the western wall opens, revealing a landscape beyond. We look upon the gateway of the West: it is in the form of two low hills tinged with the light of evening. Beyond the hills is the sea, with a path of light stretching across it.

NORTH: Lastly the door in the northern wall opens, revealing the gateway of the North. It is in the form of a low thorn hedge, with a narrow gap in it. Beyond the gap we see a cave within a great wall of rock. Deep within the shadows of the cave we see a faint glow of silver-white light, like starlight.

We will enter each of the four gates in turn, beginning with the gate of the East.

The Vision of Gorias in the East

From the East we feel a brisk wind and hear faintly the sound of horns blowing. We step up to the two stones, and pass directly between them. Now we find ourselves upon a rolling grassy plain. The wind blows strongly in our face, and all round us long grass waves and ripples in the pale dawn-light. Looking for the source of the light, in the East ahead of us we see a line of shapes silhouetted against the horizon, standing up out of the grass.

We feel drawn towards these shapes, and pause for a moment to dedicate our journey to the task of seeking and finding the mysterious city of Gorias, where the sacred sword of the Underworld is held.

Now we begin to walk forwards to the East, and as we step through the long grass our sight of the shapes upon the horizon becomes clear: we realize that we are walking towards a collection of standing stones. As we approach, we see an avenue of stones, with its entrance directly upon our path. It leads into a triple stone circle of single upright stones.

As we enter the avenue of stones, we see that the long grass grows right up to them, and it seems that the way has not been walked before us, for there is no track, no trampled grass. But when we look behind, we see that we have left no trail in the grass ourselves. We look back once more and see far away to the West two tiny upright stones amid the vast plain, marking the gate through which we entered.

Now we walk down the avenue of stones, and hear the wind seethe and mutter around them. From the outermost ring of stone ahead of us a fluting sound rises and falls in long sliding tones. The wind plays its music upon the stones, and we wonder if this is the source of the sound of horns blowing that we heard before we entered the gateway of the East.

As we enter the outermost ring of stones, we realize that they are low, not much higher than the height of a man. Each stone is carved with spirals and shallow cup-marks, and we see that no stone is similar to any other. Each spiral, each hollow, conveys a wordless message to us, and we turn to the left and walk around the circle, between the first and second row of stones. As we walk we each feel drawn towards one stone of the middle circle, and pause at that stone, wherever it may be. This is your stone companion, your life-stone in the East, and you commune with it in silence. [*Silent pause here.*]

Now we emerge from our communion with the stones, and hear again the fluting sliding sound of the wind blowing . . . it seems now to come from the innermost circle of stones, and we look towards this. There are four huge rough stones with no carving upon them, and we step into the circle between the second and the innermost ring of stones. As we do so we feel a strong current flowing around the circle, as if we wade through deep water. The sound of the wind stops suddenly, and we enter the innermost circle in silence. It is empty.

As we look upon the circle of grass, in the silent light of perpetual dawn, we see the tip of a sword showing through the earth in the very centre of the circle. It has a polished green blade, and only a short length is visible. We stand around the circle, and feel the rough stones at our backs. It seems impossible to draw closer to the sword, as if the air resists us and the earth will not carry us. We long to know the mystery of the buried sword, rising up out of the earth, and meditate in silence upon it. [*Silent pause here.*]

Over the sword we see now a shape forming, slowly, seeming to mould out of the air and light. It is the guardian of the mystery of Gorias, the city of the East. As this figure appears we are aware also of other presences in the stone circle, as if a great host has assembled invisibly while we have meditated upon the sword. One by one we approach the guardian, and seek the answer to a question. [*Pause here.*]

Now we must return to the outer world, and leave the sacred sword, its guardian and the city of the East. We slowly step out of the innermost circle, and as we do so the presence of the guardian and the invisible host instantly ceases; they vanish suddenly as if they had never been present. One by one we find our stones in the second circle, and feel the carvings on each stone, trying to understand its story and why we were drawn to it when we entered.

Now we walk swiftly down the stone avenue, and out into the grassy plain. As we leave the outermost circle of stones, we hear the wind fluting and blowing behind us, in rising and falling sliding tones, like the blowing of unearthly horns. Once again we hear the sound of a great host gathering and murmuring in the stones, moving, whispering, crying sudden, wild, short cries. We know that we must not look back, but head resolutely for the gateway into the human world.

The two gate-stones are before us, and a huge wind rises at our backs and

seems to blow us through. We pass between the stones and find ourselves in a chamber with four doors. Here we pause and slowly return to our starting place, a familiar room in the human world. Gradually the image of the chamber with four doors dissolves, and we open our eyes to return to our outer awareness.

Note: At this point there should be a break, and an opportunity to write notes. Writing the contents of the visualization out in a notebook often brings through material that might otherwise be forgotten. It is also useful for a group to discuss or share experiences after each of the four Visions, but discussions should not be interpretative or psychological, as this will lessen the impact of the experience through attempting to rationalize it. Simple acceptance and writing of notes gradually builds into a body of understanding symbols and regular patterns of experience within the faery realm. The experiences should always be accepted as themselves, not as analogues or allegories or something to be rationalized. After practice with each of the Four Cities, we may begin to experience the full cycle without a break. This is the most demanding and most potent and rewarding way of using the visualization. With silent pauses it can take more than one hour.

The Vision of Finias in the South

We begin by building strongly in our inner vision the Four Directions of North, East, South and West. In the North is night and winter; in the East is dawn and spring; in the South is noon and midsummer; in the West is autumn and evening.

As we build our vision of the Directions, we see once again the room in which we sit change into a square chamber, with a door in the wall of each Quarter, and know that we must pass through each door in turn to reach the Four Cities of the faery realm: Gorias in the East, Finias in the South, Murias in the West, and Falias in the North. We have already travelled to the city of Gorias in the East, and brought back with us keys to the power and meaning of that place. Now we will affirm each of the cities in turn, and travel to the South.

EAST: First the door in the eastern wall opens, revealing a familiar sight beyond. We look upon the gateway of the East: it is in the form of two standing stones, with a narrow gap between them. Through this gap we see a spring landscape, lit by pale blue and green light. This is the realm of the east where the city of Gorias stands in perpetual dawn.

SOUTH: Next the door in the southern wall opens, revealing a landscape beyond. We look upon the gateway of the South: it is in the form of two trees, one of green spreading branches and the other a tree of flame, constantly burning but never consumed. As we look upon these trees, they seem to exchange with one another; first one is of flame then of green branches, then the other. We look between them and see a brilliantly lit land, with a distant hill rising directly in the centre of our line of sight.

WEST: Now the door in the western wall opens, revealing a landscape beyond. We look upon the gateway of the West: it is in the form of two low hills tinged with the light of evening. Beyond the hills is the sea, with a path of light stretching across it.

NORTH: Lastly the door in the northern wall opens, revealing the gateway of the North. It is in the form of a low thorn hedge, with a narrow gap in it. Beyond the gap we see a cave within a great wall of rock. Deep within the shadows of the cave we see a faint glow of silver-white light, like starlight.

Our intention is to travel to the city of Finias, the white city of perpetual summer in the South. We focus our attention upon the door of the South, and stepping through it find ourselves before two tall trees, one of green leaves and branches, the other of brilliant orange, white and red flames. As we look upon the trees, the image reverses, with the flames and green leaves interchanging. We feel a snap of energy pulsing through us as the image changes. To enter the summer land before us we must each step through the trees exactly as the pulse of energy changes from flames to green leaves.

We count the pulse of the transformations and discover that it exchanges every nine heartbeats. On the ninth beat we step through, one by one. As we step through and the polarity of the trees exchanges, we feel a powerful surge of energy coursing through our bodies, and emerge into a brilliantly lit warm, summer place.

The full light of a high summer noon fills this land, and the air is warm and rich with the scent of flowers. We hear the hum of bees, and feel the vibrancy of the plants around us. The landscape is rolling and filled with flowering plants, bushes and many aromatic herbs. Directly before us is a hill, and a faint trail wanders through the flowers toward it. The trail meanders and curves around small trees and clusters of flowering plants, and as we walk we feel the warmth of the land through our feet. The perfume of the plants is intoxicating. As we walk the meandering path we feel exhilarated, and begin to see flashes of colour from the plants, as if a new level of sight, a new perception of light, has come to us.

Now the path divides into three, before a small flowering tree growing out of a cluster, a cairn, of coloured stones. The path to our left leads away through the rolling landscape towards a flat plain far in the distance. This side of the cairn is marked by green stones, and the road leads to Gorias by a way which we may not travel at this time.

The path to our right curves steeply way over the gentle hills and out of sight. This side of the cairn is made of blue stones, and the road leads to Murias by a way which we may not travel at this time. The path before us, just to the right of the flowering tree and cairn of coloured stones, leads to the hill. This is the way to the city of Finias which we must travel. The stones of this side of the cairn are white where the path passes. As we step forward we see that the stones facing North, the direction that we have come from, are black.

Before us the hill rises and the path begins to spiral around it, gradually climbing to the top. The crown of the hill is wreathed in a white glowing cloud, through which we see tall dim shapes. As we slowly climb the hill, we see that there is a great circle of trees upon its summit, and the white glowing cloud resolves itself into silver leaves and white blooms. Yet even as we look the sight dissolves again into a glowing white cloud. Climbing higher we look upon the land below, and see in the distant West the light shining upon the sea. In the distant East we see a flat plain and upon the horizon, an impossible distance away, the faint sight of upright stones. It is as if our vision is enhanced by the light of this place, and we can see for great distances, and perceive subtle colours and the very life essence of the trees and plants.

Now we reach the top of the hill and find ourselves standing before a grove of tall slender trees. They are similar to poplar trees, but have silver-grey bark and white and pale green and silver leaves, with many white flowers. The trees sway back and forward gently, filling the air with a rustling sound and a faint but potent perfume. Within the centre of the grove the hilltop is flat, with closely cropped grass of a brilliant silvery green.

We pause here and affirm our intent to pass within and seek out the mystery of Finias, city of the South. [*Short silent pause here.*]

Before we enter the grove we must walk around its perimeter, and as we do so we are each drawn to one of the trees. From the tree that you are drawn to, a being steps. This is your tree companion in the south, and you may only step into the sacred grove with your companion. The tree companion touches you on your shoulder, and you commune in silence with one another. [*Silent pause here.*]

The great trees sway and hiss as if there is a wind, yet we feel no breeze. The brilliant light shines like the Sun at midsummer, hot and vital, yet there is no Sun in the sky. With our companion beings, we step through into the sacred grove. Immediately the hissing sound increases until it fills the air, and we hear faint whispers, voices, sounds of movement all round us. We slowly walk around the perimeter of the grove, each guided by a companion, and look towards the centre. Where we had previously seen only grass, there now appears a white staff, set upright in the ground. We approach it slowly, and see that it has green buds as if it is about to break into leaf. Yet it is marked with a spiralling pattern, as if it is both crafted and living at the same time. As we move towards the centre of the circle, the noise around us stills and there is a powerful feeling of expectancy, of being watched, of waiting for a wonder.

Now we stand before this living staff, and about it a cloudy shape

appears. This is the guardian of the mystery of the staff, and we commune
with this being in silence. [*Silent meditation here, music if possible.*]

To each of us the guardian gives a gift, which we look upon and keep
safe. Now our tree companions bid us leave the sacred grove and gently
turn us around, each one guiding us towards the tree that has chosen us. As
we reach the trees we hear a sound of murmuring conversation and the
music of harps, high singing tones are uttered, and many voices merge in a
strange harmony. Our companions make it clear that we must not turn and
look back, but push us out of the tree circle towards the path that leads
down the hill.

Upon the summit of the hill of the South, the white city of Finias, we look
again to the East and the West, and now look for the first time to the North.
The path spirals down the hill, and we see it leading away across the rolling
countryside towards a gate of roaring flames, and beyond that gate we see
blackness. This is the way that we must travel back to the human world.

Our descent of the hill is rapid, and we reach the dividing of the ways.
From out of the little flowering tree a voice whispers one word to each of us,
and we pause to remember what is said. [*Pause here.*]

Now we make our way to the gateway, and the image of roaring flames
resolves into two trees, each alternating flames and green leaves at great
speed. As we approach we lose our exalted sight and sense of ecstasy that
has filled us in the summer land, and the rate of interchange between the
trees slows until it reaches one change every nine heartbeats. One by one
we step through into the blackness beyond, and emerge into a plain
chamber with four doors. The door behind us closes and we dissolve the
vision of the chamber, returning to a familiar room, ready to emerge into the
outer world of human life.

The Vision of Murias in the West

We begin by building strongly in our inner vision the Four Directions of
North, East, South and West. In the North is night and winter; in the East is
dawn and spring; in the South is noon and midsummer; in the West is
autumn and evening.

As we build our vision of the Directions, we see once again the room in
which we sit change into a square chamber, with a door in the wall of each
Quarter, and know that we must pass through each door in turn to reach the
Four Cities of the faery realm: Gorias in the East, Finias in the South, Murias
in the West, and Falias in the North. We have already travelled to the cities
of Gorias in the East and Finias in the South, and brought back with us keys
to the power and meaning of those places. Now we will affirm each of the
cities in turn, and travel to the West.

EAST: First the door in the eastern wall opens, revealing a familiar sight
beyond. We look upon the gateway of the East: it is in the form of two

standing stones, with a narrow gap between them. Through this gap we see a spring landscape, lit by pale blue and green light. This is the realm of the East where the city of Gorias stands in perpetual dawn.

SOUTH: Next the door in the southern wall opens, revealing a familiar landscape beyond. We look upon the gateway of the South: it is in the form of two trees, one of green spreading branches and the other a tree of flame, constantly burning but never consumed. As we look upon these trees, they seem to exchange with one another; first one is of flame then of green branches, then the other. We look between them and see a brilliantly lit land, with a distant hill rising directly in the centre of our line of sight.

WEST: Now the door in the western wall opens, revealing a landscape beyond. We look upon the gateway of the West: it is in the form of two low hills tinged with the light of evening. Beyond the hills is the sea, with a path of light stretching across it.

NORTH: Lastly the door in the northern wall opens, revealing the gateway of the North. It is in the form of a low thorn hedge, with a narrow gap in it. Beyond the gap we see a cave within a great wall of rock. Deep within the shadows of the cave we see a faint glow of silver-white light, like starlight.

It is now our intention to travel to the West, to the city of Murias. We turn to look upon the western door, and the vision of a sea lit golden-red between two low hills. We pass through the door, and immediately find ourselves in a shallow valley between two low hills. We see the water glowing with a light like sunset, yet cannot see the Sun. A stream runs through the valley and we follow it towards the sea. As we walk we hear a faint music, the sound of harps playing by the sea. The air has a salt taste to it, and we can hear the quiet breaking of waves upon the beach. As we travel through the valley, we see that there are many white stones among the grass and, looking closely, realize that these are lumps of quartz. The grass is of a rich green-blue colour, tough and springy, and there are spears of wild asparagus growing out of the sandy earth. It seems as if the sea sometimes rises and floods the valley, for the earth is mixed with sand and shells.

As we look at the valley floor, we realize that the stream is flowing towards us: it flows from the sea up into the valley. We pause to meditate on this flowing water, and as we pause we see a fish dart through the water, heading rapidly towards the sea. [Pause here.]

One by one we bend to drink from the stream: the water is pure and clear, and has no taste of salt. We walk forward, and suddenly emerge onto the shore. The sea shines with golden light, but the waves breaking upon the shoreline are rich, dark green and blue. We feel the sea, sensing its power and its presence, and pause to affirm our intent to find the hidden city of Murias. [Pause here.]

Once again the sound of music rises, as if coming out of the water, and we see two figures appear, one to our right, one to our left. They are tall with long flowing green and white hair: each plays a small, richly ornamented harp. Their fingers are long and they have golden nails. As the harpers play we follow the stream towards the sea, passing between the harpers.

Now we approach the water's edge, and as we do so the sea changes and we can look into it. The shore slopes away into the depths and we can still see the stream, now widening into a great river, flowing out of the depths of the sea towards us. As if the water has become our natural element, we walk out and it passes over our heads. We breathe water like air, and find that we are following a wide silver river over a rolling countryside. Great streams of green seaweed roll and surge about us, and we feel the currents of the invisible sea.

Far ahead we see the river emerging out of a complex towering set of pinnacles, falling in a silver cloud towards the sandy floor and gathering to flow up the land. We realize that this is the city of Murias, and pause in silence to focus our attention upon it: the towering pinnacles of glowing white and green rock, the falling silver waterfall. As we look we see shimmering movement in and out of the pinnacles, yet have no clear sight of who or what swims there. [Short pause here.]

We find that as we have contemplated the city, we have floated rapidly towards it. The rock rises directly before us, a translucent white and green complex of spires, pinnacles, caverns, fluted shapes sculpted by water. There is great movement all round us and we hear the faint sound of harps and voices.

A narrow stair in the green rock leads up to a cave mouth, and from this cave the silver river falls. One by one we climb the narrow steps, and pass in through the cave.

The cavern is filled with a huge bowl of green rock, a vast vessel with silver water bubbling up out of it, pouring over the rim and flowing away out of the cave mouth. This is the sacred vessel of the West, in the city of Murias. As we watch a presence hovers over the water, and we look upon the guardian of the cauldron of regeneration. [Pause here for contemplation. Harp music if possible.]

To each of us a faery being comes, rising out of the great vessel of stone. They bring us each a small gift, and we in turn find something that we brought with us and give it to them. These gifts appear suddenly in our hands and we recognize them, even though we had not realized that we carried them with us. With the exchange of gifts, our companions take our hand and bring us to the edge of the vessel. The rising silver water floods over the lip of the vessel, and for a moment we are touched by the flying drops of spray. As soon as this touch has been received, we are led back to the cavern mouth. There, a tiny round boat is moored, tied by a strand of braided weed to a lump of rock. The companions laughingly sign that we must enter this boat, and as soon as we do so they cast off the mooring. The tiny coracle shoots forwards with great speed and over the edge of the waterfall.

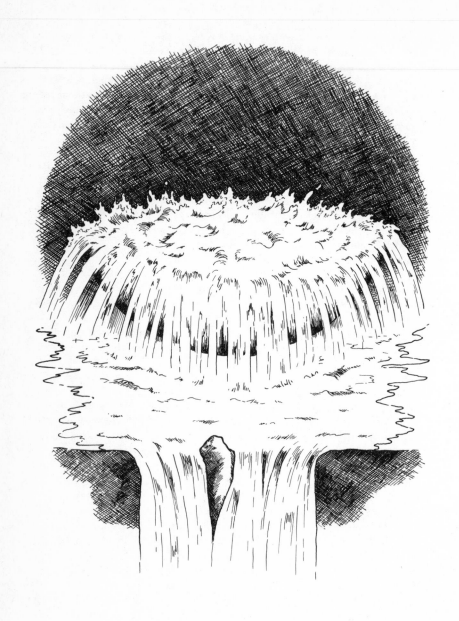

But we do not fall: the boat rises gently over the silver river and floats towards the high horizon, which we realize is the shoreline. We feel many beings swimming with us, laughing, singing, and sometimes they flash for a moment into our vision and out again. Suddenly we rise through the rolling waves, and find that our boat is floating on the surface. It comes to the shore and we step out by the silver river. Where the green harpers appeared there are two low bushes of grey-green colour. We pass between them and they rustle in the gentle wind. We cast long shadows before us, yet when we turn we see the golden path across the waters, but no Sun.

Now we pass rapidly up the valley and the river narrows into a tiny fast-flowing stream, flowing impossibly up the slope. We see before us a small dolmen, upright stones with a capstone over them. Much of it is covered by sandy earth, but there is a large opening into which the stream flows. We step into this chamber, and find ourselves passing through a door into a square chamber. We return to our outer world and the chamber dissolves, changing into the familiar place where we began our journey.

The Vision of Falias in the North

We begin by building strongly in our inner vision the Four Directions of North, East, South and West. In the North is night and winter; in the East is dawn and spring; in the South is noon and midsummer; in the West is autumn and evening.

As we build our vision of the Directions, we see the room in which we sit change into a square chamber, with a door in the wall of each Quarter, and know that we must pass through each door in turn to reach the Four Cities of the faery realm: Gorias in the East, Finias in the South, Murias in the West and Falias in the North. We have already travelled to the cities of Gorias in the East, Finias in the South and Murias in the West, and brought back with us keys to the power and meaning of those places. Now we will affirm each of the cities in turn, and travel to the North.

EAST: First the door in the eastern wall opens, revealing a familiar landscape beyond. We look upon the gateway of the East: it is in the form of two standing stones, with a narrow gap between them. Through this gap we see a spring landscape, lit by pale blue and green light.

SOUTH: Next the door in the southern wall opens, revealing a familiar landscape beyond. We look upon the gateway of the South: it is in the form of two trees, one of green spreading branches and the other a tree of flame, constantly burning but never consumed. As we look upon these trees, they seem to exchange with one another; first one is of flame then of green branches, then the other. We look between them and see a brilliantly lit land, with a distant hill rising directly in the centre of our line of sight.

WEST: Now the door in the western wall opens, revealing a familiar land and seascape beyond. We look upon the gateway of the West: it is in the form of two low hills tinged with the light of evening. Beyond the hills is the sea, with a path of light stretching across it.

NORTH: Lastly the door in the northern wall opens, revealing the gateway of the North. It is in the form of a low thorn hedge, with a narrow gap in it. Beyond the gap we see a cave within a great wall of rock. Deep within the shadows of the cave we see a faint glow of silver-white light, like starlight.

It is our intention to pass through the northern gate, to the city of Falias. We build the vision of the place beyond the door, and step through the doorway to stand before a low thorn hedge. It is of aged, thick thorn bushes, wild and uncut. The branches are black and tangled and we see only a narrow gap, with branches interlaced over it. Through this gap there is a wall of pale rock, with a narrow cave mouth, like a jagged crack. A faint silver light glows and fades from this cave.

As we bend to squeeze through the thorn gap, a sense of presence meets us and someone steps out from behind the hedge, barring our way with crossed hands, palms outwards. One by one we step up to this warden and state that we have been in Gorias, in Finias, and in Murias, and that now we seek the city of Falias and the sacred stone within it. One by one he lets us enter, but should he turn anyone back, they must await a further journey and seek admission again.

We come through the narrow gap in the hedge, and find that we are in a midnight land. The air is cold and our breath steams. Before us is a high wall of pale rock, rising up to a towering cliff far above. We see a thick band of stars in the sky, unlike any sky or constellation that we have ever seen. The gate-warden points to the jagged cave entrance, which now seems totally dark. If we seek the city of Falias and the sacred faery stone, we must enter this shadowy gate.

Now we step through into the cave, and as we do so we feel hands pull at us and turn us around several times, until we lose our sense of direction. There is no entrance to be seen, and in the dark of the cave we hear soft laughter and the sound of footfalls echoing away into the depths. We pause in the blackness, and realize that it is filled with peace, with stillness, with perfect poise. [*Silent meditation here.*]

We affirm that our intent is to travel North, seeking Falias, and even as we do so a faint light appears which we immediately follow. We feel that the floor of the cavern slopes downwards, yet it is easy to walk and we have no sense of unease.

Following the faint glowing light, we walk down and down until we feel the massive presence of the Earth, of the aged rock, all around us. Now the way narrows until we have to squeeze through, with the smooth rocks touching us on either side. The walls close in until they meet one another, and we stand before a dimly lit niche in which a small clay lamp burns before a round, polished stone mirror. The faint reflected glow flickers and fades as the lamp flame moves with the air that we have disturbed. There seems no way forward. One by one we look into the small stone mirror, and see reflected there a truth about ourselves. [*Pause for silent contemplation here.*]

Having looked within the mirror of the North, we now see the passageway with new vision. The walls leading to the niche have a fine gap, a hairline seam, and we realize that the lamp and mirror are set in a doorway. Even as we realize this, the stone door, with its lamp and tiny mirror, swings silently aside and we step through into a vast cavern.

We feel a great open space, so immense that we cannot see the far walls or the roof. The floor is of smooth polished stone, with a complex interlaced pattern set into it in faintly glowing white lines. Like a huge maze, this pattern leads us further into the cavern, and we follow it forward.

Now we see another light source, first faint, then more clearly. It radiates from a cluster of rocks rising up from the floor of the cavern. They are of white with flashes of crystalline colour, and the centre of this cluster is a tall, smooth, white stone, resting upon the natural rock outgrowths. As we approach this central place, we hear the sound of stone beating upon stone, in a deep muted resonance, rising up from all about us. A figure takes shape slowly, forming like a cloud over the smooth white stone. As we reach the rocky growths, we look fully upon the face of the guardian of the North, keeper of the sacred stone. [*Pause for communion here.*]

To each of us comes a stone being, who looks deep into our eyes, seeming to read our entire nature. Each stone being holds a fragment or shaped piece of different coloured stone, and we accept these gifts. They sign that we must place them at the foot of the white central stone, and there we see a pile of offerings: tiny coloured stones, fragments of hair, feathers, rings, ancient jewels, dried leaves. As we look the precious objects turn to leaves and feathers, while the feathers and leaves turn to silver and gold. The guardian of the sacred stone laughs at our perceptions, and we feel a deep wisdom and joy in that laugh.

As we look upon the tall white stone, resting in the centre of the rocky crystalline cluster, we see a faint shape within it. It seems to be a sleeping figure, and we look closely at this wonder. [*Silent pause here.*]

Now the guardian of the North bids us leave, and the stone beings usher us away, not in the direction by which we came but to the other side of the sacred place. They march us towards a flight of steps rising up over a rocky outcrop, lit by tiny glowing lights that seem to burn without flame or smoke, illumination coming directly out of the stone. High above us, we see a gap in the wall of the cavern. We climb the stairs and as we rise, we see three tiny images far away, high in the walls of the cavern. One is a window onto the East, the second is a window onto the South, the third is a window onto the East. We are climbing towards the window of the North.

As we climb we see the sacred stone far below emit waves of white light, and hear again the pulsing sound of stone rubbing on stone, overlaid with flowing tones and resonances. As we reach the top of the stair, we hear a great procession passing by far below, yet see nothing. Our stone companions have left us and we stand before a simple wooden shutter. One of us opens this, and it reveals a familiar room with four doors. We pass through, and the wooden door closes behind us.

Now our journey to the city of Falias in the North is complete, and we pass out of the fourfold chamber, back into the room where we began our Vision. We return slowly to outer consciousness, bringing with us the power of the Light within the Earth.

7. The Weaver Goddess in the Underworld

Our last visualization returns us to the Dark Goddess of the Underworld. In this we pass beyond the faery realm to one of the deep Underworld temples. Serious undertakings in inner transformation, magic, call it what we will, cannot be approached or achieved without experience of two closely related concepts; the Underworld and the Goddess. Although we have used the word *concepts* the Underworld and the Goddess are not theories but fundamental universal powers. They are presentations or modulations of the unknowable One Being, the ultimate reality and truth beyond expression.

There are many ways of expressing the Underworld and the Goddess, but no amount of discussion replaces actual experience. It is pointless to argue over the 'reality' of words and images, for they all derive from a deeper reality, beyond form.

Both primal concepts and powers, Goddess and Underworld, have been ignored and suppressed with terrible, possibly irreparable, effect upon both humanity and the planet Earth. Understanding the Goddess leads us to sexual balance and maturity upon all levels of consciousness, including those that transcend gender. Understanding of the Underworld brings a conscious relationship between humankind and the land, environment and planet. As the Goddess dwells within the Underworld, we should not separate the two in our imagination.

The Goddess and the Underworld represent energies and consciousness essential to our individual, collective and manifest well-being. Moreover, these two concepts and powers have the potential to rebalance our humanity and our collective world, both of which are in immediate undeniable danger of extinction. In very basic terms we may see the nuclear problem, both civil and military, as a result of ignorance and abuse of Underworld powers; Pluto and Uranus. The heavy metals are Underworld entities or stellar entities, but specifically stellar entities within the Earth. We may see the grotesque extremes of materialism and male stereotypical (rather than archetypical) consciousness as a result of suppression of Goddess powers.

The Underworld tradition, the Light within the Earth (as opposed to theoretical magic or literary occultism) must work with Goddess power. This much was realized by the revival occultists of the nineteenth and early twentieth centuries, just as it had been understood by the adepts of the Rosicrucian movement, the alchemists, and the Renaissance magicians and metaphysicians.

Only one or two generations ago, Goddess workings were unusual in magical groups, though not unknown. Magical arts were still dominated by savage phantoms of male egocentric 'authority' and dogmatic 'hierarchy', phantoms which have by no means been exorcized at the present time. Such male-dominated groups tended and still tend to work with the Goddess only in her Venus or sexual-loving aspect, because this is close to the pernicious stereotype of pseudo-femininity to which they were conditioned from childhood.

As we emerge from a period of monosexual religion and culture, such stereotypical imagery is beginning to be replaced by something new, yet essentially ancient and primal and enduring.

Social conditions change slowly, and often express transformations which were once limited to exploration by magical groups of earlier generations. Thus, the restoration of sexual equality is now a widespread social and political issue in the Western world whereas at the turn of the century, equality was often a highly daring experiment in which men and women worked magic together (as opposed to the exclusively male Masonic Orders from which such groups often derived). More significant than the mere fact that men and women were working equally at magical arts, though this was a major step forward in itself, were Goddess-orientated rituals and visualizations that began to appear, often drawing on material from earlier cultures and religions. The late Dion Fortune, for example, spent an entire life in the task of resolving Atlantean and Egyptian Goddess forces in the context of the twentieth century. The results, with many potent Goddess visions and rituals, are found not in her textbooks on psychology and magic (which seem outdated now) but in her remarkable novels.

Further discussions of the explosion of Goddess worship and various aspects of active feminism in revival paganism are not relevant in a book of this sort; nevertheless, one of the most astonishing of the many wonders appearing in the twentieth century is the irresistible return of the Goddess, regardless of her forms of expression. Only a generation ago students heard whispered secrets concerning 'sex magic' in which something unspeakably mysterious occurred between men and women (and it was not sexual intercourse!). The entire science of polarity magic has now opened out and is becoming increasingly defined and intelligible. Such developments could not occur, in the magical or poetical sense, without the active power of the Goddess restoring our awareness to a balanced condition.

In Western esoteric tradition, as in the East, there is a wide range of what are nowadays called *feminine archetypes*. They are preserved in legend, myth, folklore and in magical, alchemical and mystical allegory, including the heretical Grail legends. Such archetypes have been banished, often unsuccessfully, from political orthodox religion, though they frequently resurface in the form of female saints who replace pagan goddesses, or as folklore and popular superstition, and revivals of the cult of the Virgin Mary.

More important than any of the sources listed is the inner tradition of making contact with empowered images of goddesses, through meditation, visualization and ritual. It is quite facile and inaccurate to suggest that the West has no goddesses and that such images can play no part in mystical or magical work; but a clear definition and firm contact with such images is often difficult to establish, due to centuries of orthodox suppression and conditioning. Once the contacts have been made, however, the Goddess is an undeniable force, and experienced as a powerful presence in many ways.

In the Underworld tradition there are two aspects of the Goddess that are especially relevant and potent. We might call them She Who Dwells Below, the Goddess of the Underworld, the Dark Mother, and She Who Dwells Above, the universal Goddess of the Stars. They are extremes of one unity, and are found in practical terms to be very close to one another when we visualize or meditate upon them; but they are not interchangeable in a facile manner through human arbitration.

The Western tradition has a *shortened way* to enlightenment, which has much in common with similar methods found in Tibetan Buddhism or Zen, though there is no suggestion here that they are identical; we do not need to turn to Eastern variants when we already have well-defined and powerful initiatory techniques of our own. The similarities are due to shared properties of human consciousness; the differences are due to ancestors, environment and psychic patterns, all of which are transcended only by working with and moving through a native tradition to its very end.

The shortened way simply consists of going into the Underworld and encountering the Goddess. For many people this is a terrifying experience to be avoided at all costs: such people should not be involved in empowering traditions or initiatory arts of consciousness and energy. If they do become so involved, most soon abandon the effort or become side-tracked into the various self-perpetuating dead ends of occultism or New Age cosiness and mutual congratulation. These may seem like hard words but no growing experience, no transformation, is ever easy.

By descending into the Underworld we are paradoxically reaching towards comprehension and experience not only of the Dark Goddess, the Power of Taking and Giving, but also of Her universal stellar aspect. First the catabolic destroying force that we fear, which is the Dark Goddess, then her universal aspect beyond all concepts of self-hood or false limitation. In this phase we comprehend the Goddess as a conscious power permeating all time, space and energy.

We find the imagery for this Goddess in various forms in myth and legend, and such imagery is particularly active upon inner levels of visualization and contact. In our present context we can exclude intermediary forms such as culture goddesses, love goddesses, sister goddesses, war goddesses and specific localized female deities: these are strung like beads upon a cord that reaches from the Underworld to the Stars. During the Underworld Initiation, we realize that the linear concept of this cord is an illusion, and that both ends are one, giving us the image of a circle or sphere. This sphere contains the universe in one dimension, and the planet or Underworld in another: the Goddess weaves all dimensions and energies together.

In human terms, this power is found both beneath and within, a practical matter of the direction of energy and consciousness through ritual and imaginative constructs such as goddess forms and guided visualizations. To our ancestors there was an eminently simple method: they went underground into chambers, caves, catacombs, and sought enlightenment. This physical movement is analogous to a visionary transformative experience in which we enter a realm beneath the Earth, yet find that it is full of stars. In both Celtic and Greek mythology, we find the goddess known as The Weaver, and She appears in several important magical or mystical visions. The visualization which follows employs many elements of the Goddess tradition, showing The Weaver in one of her most potent aspects

---

The Weaver Goddess

We begin by meditating upon a single candle flame. [*A candle or slow-burning nightlight is lit here.*] We look upon this light, firstly with open eyes, and know that it represents the spiritual light that burns within us. This light is everywhere, with its origin and centre within all and any chosen time, space or being. As we meditate upon the light, we close our eyes, and remain in formless contemplation for a few moments. [*A short silent pause here.*]

Now we see before us a vision of three rings or circles, interlaced to form a sphere. One ring is vertical, one horizontal, one fully open towards us. As we look upon these rings they rotate slowly, each taking the place of the other. They seem to flow and merge into one another, and at the same time turn with their own motion. As we look upon this mystery, the rings expand and pass beyond our view moving through and over us until we are within them yet they are grown so vast that they are unseen.

We find ourselves standing upon a warm, sunny square or courtyard. The air is scented with summer perfumes from many exotic plants; we see a huge stone wall of tightly fitting massive blocks of masonry . . . a flowering tree grows up the wall, its huge white and red blooms open wide to the hot sunlight. We have never seen a tree of this type before . . . its trunk is smooth, dark green with deep black markings, and the leaves are wide and shining with a rich deep blue colour shot with grey-green tints. A tiny breeze stirs the wide white and red flowers, and they rustle gently.

With the sound of the light wind in the leaves and blossoms, we hear a faint footfall, and turn to see a boy coming towards us. He is no more than a child, dressed in a plain white tunic, as if he is a pupil or novice. He solemnly beckons to us, and leads us towards a square doorway in the wall. A plain stone slab tilts upwards to admit us to a cool dark building: we pass within and the heat and scents of summer, the perfume of the strange tree, immediately vanish. The interior of the building is cool and silent. We find that we are in a large chamber, lit by high slits near to the roof, through which shafts of dim light pass, filtered through windows or membranes that shade it pale green and blue. At the far end of this place is a wide circular well, into which a flight of steps descends. Our guide leads us with a steady formal pace towards the stairwell, and when we reach the first step, he chimes upon a small bronze bell suspended from a single carved stone shaped like the fine stem of a plant with an opening blossom.

A clear deep note sounds through the chamber, and the boy sits cross-legged beneath the stone flower and vibrating bell. We pause, and see that someone is already ascending the steps to meet us. . . .he is an old man in a long, dark red robe with a curious symbol embroidered upon it. He reaches the top of the stair, and looks carefully at each of us in turn. He holds a large ball of multicoloured twine in his hand, and suddenly throws it so that it rolls down the steps and out of sight, unwinding as it falls. We hear the soft sound of the ball passing rapidly from step to step. The old man holds the end of the twine, which he passes to one of us when the sound of the ball fades and can be heard no more. He then sits cross-legged opposite the boy, on the other side of the stairwell. We know that we must descend between them, following the line of the ball of twine.

As we descend the steps, we realize that we are climbing down into a vast cavern, so great that we cannot measure its size. It is lit by a dim radiance reflected from the walls, though we cannot see the source of the light. Our stair, which seemed so huge when we entered upon it, clings to the edge of one wall, and descends like a tiny ledge into the depths. The thread runs straight ahead of us and we follow it, loosely hand over hand, letting it lie upon the stairs behind reaching up into the chamber far above.

When we finally arrive at the foot of the long flight of steps, we find that we are standing upon a level stone floor, and that the line of twine suddenly turns, rolling away in a wide curve to our right. We follow it, and feel that we are travelling in a great circle . . . soon the wall and the stairs are left behind. Our footsteps echo back to us very faintly, seeming to come from far away, and suddenly the twine seems like a lifeline; without it we have no idea where we are going, and without it we would not be able to find our way back to the stairs. We follow the twine, and feel that we are walking in a spiral so vast that we have hardly begun to cover one turning. The roof of the cavern is lost to sight above us; looking up we seem to fall into a dizzy pit of shadow. Soft radiance seems to fill the air around us, then recedes as if breathing in and out.

As we walk we slowly become aware of a firm light, as if from a lamp or fire, and a solid shape like a black circle or disk beyond that light. Our thread leads us to this. The shape is still far away, but our movement over the smooth stone floor is rapid and steady, and the disk seems to come towards us, so huge is the surrounding space that we have no way of judging relative proportions.

As we draw closer to the disk, we see that it is made of glass or polished black stone. It is a perfect circle of reflecting blackness, many times the height of a man, seeming to float without support, balanced upon its edge which just touches the stone floor. By the side of this vast mirror is a tall silver-coloured stand shaped like an upright serpent, and from its mouth a clear flame burns. We draw closer to the mirror and the lamp, and see that the serpent stand is not of silver, but of crystal. The flame seems to appear from nowhere out of the serpent's mouth; we can see no oil or wick to supply it. In the vast black mirror, we see a reflection of ourselves, softly lit by the crystal lamp. We seem small, almost pitiful in the vast dreaming shadows of the cavern.

Looking upon the circular disk, with its glassy black polished face, we realize that within it we can see a shape, beyond our personal reflections, as if it shows something behind or beyond us. We strive to see this shape, yet it eludes us . . . the closer we look, the further away it seems to fade. We stand back and try to focus upon what is hidden in the depths of the great black mirror. As as we do so, we become aware of someone standing near to the mirror's edge, on the side opposite the crystal serpent. A figure steps into the light and we see that it is a woman in a long black robe and deep hood, who had been hidden from us in the shadows. She carries a long staff,

with a thread spiralling around it, and we feel a sense of terrible power emanating from her. She seems to glide across the floor towards us, and raise her staff high above her head: in an instant she strikes the serpent lamp, and it shatters into many pieces. We are plunged into total darkness, so complete that we seem to be falling.

As we fall we see a circle suddenly illuminated below us, and we realize that we are falling into the black mirror, which has now become light. We fall through into a rocky cave, brightly lit by many tiny lamps burning in niches and crevices all around. We tumble onto the floor, and for the moment see nothing but the stone roof and the tiny lamps. We realize that we are at the feet of a vast dark figure, and we stand to look upon it. It is a woman, towering above us, carved of black polished stone. She sits with her head tilted slightly downwards, as if looking at us. Her face is huge and calm, showing no human emotion. Her arms are outstretched, and we see that a thick strand of rope falls from one hand towards the floor, while another reaches from her other hand up into the cavern roof, where it vanishes away through the rock. Only then do we realize that she is not looking at us, but at a picture carved into the floor of the cave. The rope that descends sinks through the stone, and merges into an image of a loom, upon which we have fallen. The rope leading upwards passs through another picture of a loom carved into the roof, and we see a mirror image of the floor below, with tiny spirals and shapes in the weaving.

This was the place seen in the dim image just visible in the black mirror before the breaking of the crystal serpent lamp. We pause to meditate upon the figure of the Goddess, and upon her Mystery. [*A pause for silent meditation here.*]

As we sit and meditate upon the meaning of the vast Goddess image and her double loom, a young woman in a white robe enters the cave and begins to tend the lamps: each lamp has its wick trimmed until the flame burns brightly. She pays no attention to us but as she passes round the chamber walls and tends each lamp, we feel a cleansing clarifying power at work within us. Even as she trims the lamps, the light increases, until the entire chamber is filled with brilliant illumination. The giant black Goddess figure is surrounded by a halo of light; the thick strands of twisted rope shimmer in her hands, and rotate with spiralling changes of colour. The loom pattern, inlaid into the floor where we sit, seems to move and change configuration. We look upwards to the chamber roof and see that the loom above changes also, then slowly fades away into a pattern of stars cut deeply into the stone.

We are drawn by these carved patterns of stars, in great spirals and complex shapes; we stand, and find that as we rise the black Goddess slowly fades from sight, vanishing into the brilliance of the lamps. As we reach our feet, we hear a gong chime [*gong sound here if possible*] and know that the maiden has finished trimming the lamps. As the echoes of the gong fade away, the roof of the chamber, with its patterns of stars, begins to crack open and divide into two parts. The right and left-hand halves of the roof slowly pull apart, revealing a night sky filled with shining constellations. At the very centre of this sky is a moving coil of stars, a whirlpool of light turning inwards and outwards in a double spiral.

From the surface above, a simple wooden ladder is slowly lowered down to us; we see an aged man and a child on either side of the ladder, their faces looking down at us briefly. When we begin to climb, they retreat out of our line of sight. One by one we reach the ladder top and climb to find ourselves on the summit of a high, round hill. Lamplight shines out of the hole from which we have climbed, but light from the double spiral of stars increases, moves and grows until we can see nothing else. . .

Within the centre of the spiral there is a cloudy veil shimmering and pulsing before a partly hidden figure. As the veil thins momentarily, we see a woman in a silver-grey robe, with a deep hood totally covering her face. In her hand she holds a distaff, from which a spiralling thread twists and turns until it becomes the double coil of stars. [*See the trump Judgement in the Merlin Tarot for this image.*]

The veil grows thin and without knowing why, we find that we have already bowed our heads and covered our eyes with our hands. We remain in silence and experience the power of the great Goddess as she spins, weaves and unweaves. [*Silent meditation here.*]

Now we feel a change, a movement beneath our feet as if the hilltop has tilted momentarily. The air grows warmer and is filled with strange rich scents. We sense sunlight upon our faces and when we lower our hands to look, find that we are back in the sunlit courtyard, standing by the tree with its huge blooms and strange coloured leaves. Upon the courtyard floor, we see for the first time a large woven carpet. It is coloured red, white and black, and contains many abstract patterns and connecting lines and shapes. Upon the carpet stand some stone balls, seemingly thrown at random. We feel strongly drawn to play this ball-throwing game but as we turn towards the carpet, the old priest in his red robe appears from behind the tree and forbids us to approach or touch anything, making a curious sign with his hands. We try to remember this sign, for it is part of the inner temple language. He directs us away from the carpet and its entrancing pattern and shows us instead a square low door in the wall beside the tree. The door has a thick lintel and capping stone and even as we look at it, the stone slab from which it is made tilts upwards, revealing a dimly lit familiar room. At first it looks like a shadow room within a dream, but gradually it takes on substance and colour. We pass through the stone door and sit, each in his or her familiar chair. There is a sound of grinding stone, and as the door closes our vision of the temple courtyard wall fades away. As we return to the outer world, we each discover that we have been given a token by one of the people encountered upon our journey. This token appears in our hands and we study it for a moment, immediately knowing who gave it to us and reflecting upon its meaning. These tokens will enable us to return to the inner worlds through which we have travelled in seeking the Weaver

Goddess. But as each token is different, and was given by a different guardian, we cannot know or presume where they will ultimately lead.

But is it now time to redirect our vision, and return to the outer world, bringing with us the light and the knowledge that we have gained within.

Futureword

There is much more to be done in communication and relationship with the faery realm. I hope that this book has indicated some of the ways ahead, taking ancient but living tradition and restating it for modern use.

If we remain at the level of thinking of faeries as little sprites or romanticized nature-spirits, we tacitly condone and support the destruction of the land. Fantasy is the artificial sweetener upon the poisoned cake of materialism. In the real world of the imagination, where form and energy dissolve into one another and boundaries of consciousness and self-limiting images are broken down, cosy fantasy cannot exist. There are terrors in the Underworld, in the faery realm, as well as glory and ecstasy.

While technology mindlessly reports to itself how we have upheld a century or more of pillage and violation that may not be undone, it is our living awareness that must talk to the land. If we do so the land talks back . . . and tells us that through the inner darkness there is light to be found. This light is not a fluorescent strip, a VDU, a radioactive glow, but the living light, the light that radiates redemptive and regenerative energy to all living beings.

Before we can truly receive and re-radiate this light, we must be aware of other orders of life . . . aware in a true sense of communication and exchange, not merely as scientific or biological research and experiment. We are all part of one another: many orders of life are non-material, non-organic.

It is upon this subtle level of exchange of energies that the traditions of faery and Underworld beings can be of value to us: they are not ignorant fantasies of the past, but an interlacing of statements concerning the deepest intuitions, understandings and experiences of humanity living upon and within the planet. For too long we have been dominated by the hollow monster of materialism. More recently we have taken up the equally enervating psychological world-view that all myths, Otherworld entities and non-materialist traditions are somehow rationalizations or vague graspings confined purely to the psyche of humanity, with no interaction with any other part of the holism of land, planet, universe. This is no longer sufficient, nor was it ever sufficient other than as a crude interim stage leading us away from religious dogma.

Rather than write an Afterword which sums up whatever may be concluded in this book, I prefer a Futureword. The only conclusions are the ones that you will make when you work with contacting the faery realm. The futures of humanity and the land are inseparable: the Light within the Earth is your light . . . only you can find it, and only you can hide it from yourself.

We share that light with innumerable other orders of being, the nearest subtle companions being those of the faery realm. Enough has been said in the earlier chapters of this book, and suggested in the exercises, to give some preliminary insights into their relationship with us, and our deeper relationship to the holism of the Underworld. Use your inherent ability to pass into the Underworld; it is your original home. Seek out the faery realm, and reopen the exchange between the people of that place and yourself. We have much to offer one another.

Appendix 1
Time Cycles and Working Patterns

ONE DAY CYCLE

Morning: Sacred Space and the Four Elements (see pages 42–3)
Afternoon: Basic Underworld visualization (pages 72–3)
Evening (around twilight): The Tree Below (page 78)
Midnight (if possible): Underworld Temple and Dark Goddess (page 75)

TWO DAY CYCLE

Morning One: Sacred Space and the Four Elements (as above)
Afternoon: Basic Underworld Visualization (as above)
Evening (around twilight): The Tree Below (as above)
Midnight (if possible): Underworld Temple and Dark Goddess (as above)
Morning Two: a) Sacred Space and the Four Elements
　　　　　　　　b) The Rising Light Below (page 68)
Afternoon Two: Underworld Temple and Dark Goddess: includes seeking ancestral contact
Evening Two: The Four Cities (page 87)
No late night work.

ONE WEEK CYCLE (ASSUMING FULL AVAILABILITY)

1. Sacred Space, Elements, Directions (Four sessions, one for each Direction as in Figure 2)

2. Basic Underworld visualization (Morning)
The Rising Light Below (Afternoon). Develop each phase of this exercise in turn.
The Tree Below (Evening)

3.   Sacred Space reaffirmed (Morning)
Un-narrated contact meditations on faery allies (as defined from The Tree Below on the previous day) (Afternoon)
The Tree Below (repeated) (Evening)

4.   The Rising Light Below (Morning: develop all phases)
The Underworld Temple and Dark Goddess (Afternoon)
The Four Cities (Evening)
Midnight meditation outdoors if possible

5.   a) Visit a power location or sacred site if possible. Work to *pass within* the site in visualization (pages 53–4). (Full day)
or b) Sacred Space affirmed (morning) with the intent of connecting the Four Cities to the Four Directions of the Outer world (afternoon).

6.   The Rising Light Below (Morning)
The Vision of Thomas Rhymer: improvized (see page 54) (Afternoon).
The Weaver Goddess (Evening)

7.   Sacred Space moving directly into The Rising Light Below exercises while the Sacred Space is open (Morning)
The Tree Below (Afternoon). This visualization will now spontaneously show some major changes if you allow silent pauses or improvized narrative based upon the main narrative (page 78).
The Four Cities (Evening) Improvize working this contact through movement with a ground-plan based on Figure 2. Conclude with Sacred Space
Midnight meditation (outdoors if possible)

One Month Cycle

Work with the lunar phases, always beginning at the Dark Moon. You work as follows: DARK/WAXING/FULL/WANING. The Dark Moon in week four allows for a period of rest. Devise your own working pattern based initially on the material in this book. If time is limited, work once a day at the same time every day. Work outdoors as much as possible.

Annual Cycle

Work from November to November or February to February. Observe seasonal festivals and lunar phases. Be aware of the Directions in relationship to the Seasons. Use the guidelines above to fill in specific work patterns. Work outdoors as much as possible.

Appendix 2
Notes on Visualization in Groups

SOME TYPICAL RESPONSES IN VISUALIZATION

In practical group work with empowered visualization it is important not to predetermine or hijack the event by telling people what to expect beforehand.

My own introduction to magical visualization, in the late 1960s, was in very strict private circumstances within the Western esoteric tradition. Group visualizations and exploratory workshops and similar events, so widespread today, were virtually unknown at this time. They would have been, in any case, contrary to the strict methods by which the tradition had long been disseminated, through a simple cell-system with no public image or platform. This semi-secret approach derives from centuries of oppression rather than from any kind of elitism. On a more subtle level the containment of a magical tradition within a narrow lineage was supposed to enhance and preserve its energy and validity. I do not think that this conservative approach is valid today, though it was undoubtedly essential in the past. The restriction within the old traditions was found in many streams of initiation, ranging from faery lore preserved only within certain families, to magical groups and orders with a more formal structure. These groups were not, incidentally, the ones best popularized by modern journalism or biography.

Traditional techniques of visionary experience, regardless of their source or style, are almost always of the sink-or-swim variety. During training in primal wisdom techniques of transformation, in any part of the world, the student is given certain experiences which are in themselves the initiation, the start. If he or she fails to move, then the teaching goes no further. The next stages are usually found by asking the right questions, based upon your experiences in the empowered visualizations.

In my own case this meant that I was given no background whatsoever to the technique, no introduction to the imagery, and very little 'explanation' after the event. Negative as all this may seem in the light of developments today, it was the best possible introduction to powerful visualization, for I could not deny what happened. After all, I had not been prepared in any way or conditioned to expect specific results.

Traditionally the responsibility rests upon the student to swim or sink, and upon the experienced teacher or leader of visualization to empower the event and not hold back or trivialize anything for the unwitting student or group. When highly energized visualizations are experienced in this manner they can have a revelatory effect, not merely on the conscious mind but upon the subtle energies and transpersonal levels of awareness. Larger group workings were usually reserved for people with experience and skill, and seldom involved more than ten or twelve people.

There has been a significant change to the potential of group working in the last decade (1980–1990). I do not pretend to know what this change is or how it has come about, but some collective crossing of a threshold has made group visualization and direct experience of the inner worlds more accessible than ever before. The old traditions often teach that if enough people work successfully with changes of consciousness and energy, their transformation permeates through to us all. Certainly it is now possible to work with larger groups of people in specific empowered visualization and other techniques in a way that would have been unthinkable only twenty years ago.

I do not, by the way, subscribe to the enthusiastic theory that this change heralds a new level of human spiritual awareness ushering in the New Age; I merely accept that it has occurred during my lifetime, and welcome it. Each century, each millennium, has proclaimed the New Age . . . it is ever coming. If our enthusiasm for a New Age means that we are able to bring out the archetypal image of the sacred land and planet, and realize and manifest the Light within the Earth, then it is welcome. If, however, it is channelled into a movement of elitism and escapism, in which only the beautiful and spiritually evolved will survive through rejecting anything that does not fit with their preconceptions, then it is a subtle form of suppression.

The Tree Below

(Do not read these notes until you have done the visualization!)

Work with Underworld visualizations reveals a remarkable consistency between groups, regardless of their location or background. The Tree Below is a typical example of a visualization leading into the faery realm, and a few typical responses are worth noting. If you are engaged in practical work these responses should not be allowed to precondition any group or individual experience.

1.   The Tree Below. This image is often difficult for people, but it is the key to the entire experience. Its paradoxical aspect enables many of the transformations and experiences which follow. The most frequent comment is that people are not sure whether to climb down the tree face first, or feet first.

2.   On descending the tree, a large number of people report that their clothing or even their appearance has changed. This occurred spontaneously with various groups, and seems to be a quite independent transformation, not built into the visualization. I had not been aware of it myself, but realized that it was a significant transformation, nevertheless. Interestingly, those who reported that their clothing and appearance had changed when they descended the tree, also experienced a change back to their customary appearance when they climbed back up to the human world.

3.   The experience of the rapid walk along the grassy plain seems to be uniform, though some people find that they travel at great speed and reach the destination before it is described. This reaching forward and seeing or experiencing aspects of the visualization before they are verbalized can and does occur at any stage of the journey.

4.   The Mound. As a rule the mound is seen by all members of the group as described in the vision, but occasionally people will not see the mound, but a specific location such as a sacred hill or faery site that they know of. Often the location seen is a surprise, and not necessarily a famous site . . . though these also occur.

5.   The Guardian. The guardian seems to vary from person to person. Originally I worked with a description of a faery warrior inside the doorway, but so many people saw something different that it seemed right to change this part of the sequence to leave an independent vision. In some cases individuals saw a doorkeeper or guardian, and when I described a faery warrior their first guardian passed them on to this established figure. In other cases what was seen was quite different from my own description, and could not be reconciled with it. Usually the guardian is a being from faery tradition, though there are occasional exceptions. Sometimes the guardian or doorkeeper is associated with a

specific site. An unusual example occurred in Ireland, where one group member saw St Patrick as the guardian of the doorway into the faery mound, and the mound itself as a sacred hill associated with Patrick, to which pilgrimages are still made. Curiously the saint welcomed the traveller, and allowed him to enter the faery hall . . . not what I would have expected from such an orthodox and anti-pagan figure in Christian hagiology.

6.   Inside the Hall. Here we begin the encounter, and at this point many people saw things that were to come shortly in the guided narrative; others had quite independent experiences as soon as they entered the hall. On looking at the faery host (to our left) many people saw a wide range of beings, some human, some clearly non-human. Typical reports included the clear understanding that some members of the host welcomed our presence, while others were actively opposed to us being there.

Examples of Encounters

In group work, I have found that almost everyone will meet a faery companion or ally. The visualization on page 78 is an example of one means of doing so. In that vision, we enter a faery hall and as part of the experience, potential allies offer to work with us between the worlds; we are allowed to consider up to three companions that may come forward, but not to choose at random from among the faery host itself. Some people do not, of course, choose to accept their first, second or third potential ally.

In some cases, it seems that the first companion is often of a most desirable nature, while the second and third are more true to one's abilities or needs. A typical example was Mary (not her real name) who was offered a beautiful young poet with long flowing golden hair and playing a small harp. She was uncertain about this companion, as she felt that he was too beautiful, when a quiet dark-haired man stepped out from behind him and said, 'Take me, I'm a gardener, I'll be much more use to you in your own land'.

Brian (also a substitute name) was approached by a group of motley people who mocked him. Eventually a huge warrior-type put his arm around Brian's shoulders and bellowed, 'Take me with you . . . or are you afraid that when we get back up there people will take you for a faery?'. This second incident may seem frivolous but Brian worked in circumstances that might, occasionally, put him in physical danger from attack, hence the faery companion as joking warrior.

We must remember that these are not psychological associations or dreams, but the presentations of entities, real independent beings, to our imaginative creative vision. The relationship between faery form and our own storehouse of images is discussed on pages 36–40.

A third personal example, from someone whom we shall call Maud, is more complex. Firstly she was certain that she did not want to accept anyone, and that therefore no one would offer to be her companion while in the faery hall. To her surprise, two human beings came forward, a man and woman. They were of mature appearance, wearing white and purple robes. They asked her to take them out of faeryland and back with her to the human realm. She refused them, and they asked again. Eventually they left her, and were replaced by a tall, thin, green female with slanting eyes, one of a class of faery beings frequently reported. This faery woman said, 'Take me instead, my name is Lilith'. Maud still refused.

The green faery beings, tall, thin, with large slanted eyes and beautiful features, are ancient and enduring entities, often connected to the cycle of plant life in our world. They are particularly skilled at exchanging creative and sexual energies between themselves and other beings. Traditionally they are also said to be dangerous if insulted, mistreated or aroused to anger in any way. They are similar, in some ways, to the wood-nymphs reported in classical tradition; these were not pretty little nature spirits, but came in the form of terrifying women with rapacious appetites for love, capable of giving much and taking all from a human consort. They also protected their tree-forms savagely.

That a faery woman should say she was 'Lilith' relates to the ancient myth of Adam's first wife, Lilith, a nature goddess too wild and uncontrollable for the patriarchal Jews and their Christian heirs, and so written out of the orthodox texts. (The motif of Adam, Eve, Lilith and the faery realm occurs in a powerful visualization devised by Colonel Seymour, one of the pioneers of the revival of Celtic and Western magic in the early years of this century.)[20]

When Maud's experience was described, several group members felt, as I did, that the first two people were ancestral contacts, though others (including Maud) thought that they were people trapped in the faery realm. She had not wanted the responsibility of trying to get them out. The gist of it all, from a theoretical rather than an ethical point of view, was that she turned down a human or ancestral contact, and so came into a pure faery contact.

Appendix 3 The Six Companions

In the vast collection of folk tales (loosely called faery tales today) amassed by the Grimm brothers in nineteenth-century Denmark and Germany, there is one called *The Six Servants*. This motif is found around our world in many variants, in every culture. It involves a man or woman acquiring supernatural allies, companions or helpers. The faery tale of the Six Servants gives us an insight into the benefits conferred by faery allies upon the pure of heart. We can only deal with the barest summary of the story here, but many versions are found in collections of European folk tales, including the edited and full versions from the Grimm collection itself.

A young man (a prince) falls in love with the daughter of a vicious sorceress, who murders her daughter's suitors by beheading them when they fail the tests that she sets. The prince becomes ill for seven years when his father forbids him to court the sorceress's daughter. Eventually the father gives way, and on the road to the sorceress's hall, the young man encounters six companions, who offer to be his servants. They are most unusual beings.

The first is, when he chooses, of immense size with an unlimited appetite. The second can hear all that passes in the world, even the grass growing. The third is very long, and can make himself three thousand times as long and tall as the highest mountain. The fourth has to keep a cover over his eyes, as the power of his glance shatters everything he looks upon. The fifth grows colder as the weather grows hotter . . . on ice he cannot breathe for the heat, in the middle of a furnace he freezes bitterly. The sixth has a long neck and keen eyes that can see to the very end of the world. Each of these companions helps the young man to gain his love, by using their special abilities to overcome the tests and tricks of the sorceress. (Please read the rest of the tale for yourself!)

These six companions or servants are of typical classes or types of faery being widely reported. Four of them are consistent with Robert Kirk's descriptions of faery tradition in seventeenth century Scotland: the great-eater (1), the shattering-sight (4), the power of opposites (cold when hot, winter when summer and so forth) (5), and of course the far-sighted (6).

In faery magic and the Underworld tradition of Northern and Western European shamanism, allies of this sort were frequently sought. In the folk tale, they lend their help for a good cause, that of a young man's love against the evil magic of a sorceress. When he and his lover are married, the companions take their leave 'at the church door', saying that he has no further need of them. This is a typical teaching: the companions each appeared voluntarily along the road which the young man took, even though he knew that his adventure might lead to his death. They helped him through many tests and trials, and when he married his true love, departed.

The deepest levels of the tale are a spiritual drama concerning the soul and its harmony or partnership of masculine and feminine forces. It may be taken as an initiatory narrative (the road leading to possible death, the acquiring of supernatural allies, the tests set by the Dark Mother, the liberation of the Lover, and marriage of polarities). The union of male and female causes the companions to leave, for what happens next is upon a new cycle of realization.

Appendix 4
The Vision of Thomas Rhymer

(from *The Underworld Initiation*)

Thomas the Rhymer, also known as Lord Learmont, Thomas of Ercledoune and 'True Thomas', lived during the thirteenth century. He is an extremely important person in the exposition of the hidden tradition, and forms one of a number of historical persons who may be termed Justified Men. These individuals are not necessarily connected in any fraternal manner, least of all by the spurious nonsense about 'secret orders' that has been forced into commercial popularity in recent years. They are connected through time, however, by a common thread of purpose and symbolic lore.

In magical terms, they are the prophets and teaching masters of the secret Tradition, and may be said to exist metaphysically as a united body of consciousness which has expressed itself through specific members in serial time. Active magical groups who perpetuate genuine oral teaching traditions have various inner-world contacts whom they claim to be members of such a body. These are not, incidentally, mysterious immortals residing in seclusion in the Andes or on Mars, but are the conscious resonance or echo of certain advanced souls who are supposed to be concerned with the problems and spiritual development of those who are their children in outer time.

Whether or not one accepts this more recondite theory is a matter of indifference, for there are sufficient historical Justified Men within the narrow confines of British tradition, and they have left words, songs, poems and music behind, whereby those who follow in their footsteps through the Underworld may be guided.

The list includes the Reverend Robert Kirk of Aberfoyle, Geoffrey of Monmouth, and the anonymous author of the Grail legends, while in more modern times we might include the authors George MacDonald and Charles Williams.

Not all metaphysicians or acclaimed philosophers or holy men belong to this grouping, for not all wisdom is gained through the Underworld. The reader should be familiar by now with the hallmarks of the Underworld tradition as suggested, and will be able to find clues in the works of great thinkers and metaphysicians. He or she will also be surprised at the absence of such clues in the works of apparently reputed representatives of Western religion, ethics and philosophy.

Thomas of Ercledoune, therefore, was renowned as a prophet during his own lifetime (and in his own country), and printed versions of his accurate predictions were circulated after his death, some still active as late as the nineteenth century. His pre-vision was the result of the Underworld Initiation, gained by his relationship with the Faery Queen, as described in the famous old ballads and the Romance text which bear his name.

Thomas is also said to be the author of the earliest version of 'Tristram and Iseult', and may be rightly said to have had a far-reaching effect upon literature and upon the common imagination for the last seven hundred years. During the nineteenth century, his published prophecies caused Englishmen to flee to the hills in fear of an imminent disaster – which, unlike many of his quite accurate predictions, did not occur.

Living during the time of Robert the Bruce and William Wallace, with whom he was associated, Thomas is thought to have been a nationalist agent. This political role of the magus is found frequently throughout history. During Edward the First's bloody ravaging of Scotland, Thomas seems to have been an active traveller and seer in the nationalist cause.

Two traditions of his death are extant. The first is that he was murdered for political reasons by the followers of the Earl of March, and that he foresaw his death accurately. The second is that he lives on in the hollow Eildon hills of his home region in the Lowlands. Like Merlin, or Arthur, Thomas wears the mantle of the national hero who is also attuned to a deep and powerful myth; politics and magic are woven together in his cloak.

The large estates of Ercledoune were donated to the Church by Thomas's son, also called Thomas, thus fulfilling one prediction. The magical hawthorn tree of Thomas's initiation lived on until 1814, when it was blown down in a gale. The local people of Earlston on the River Leader, about thirty-five miles from Edinburgh, naturally attempted its revival by pouring whisky upon the roots, but to no avail. Thomas had prophesied that 'As long as the Thorn Tree stands,/ Ercledoune shall keep its lands.' In that same year, six hundred years after these words were set down, a chain of financial disasters struck the community, and all common land was sold in payment of debts.

William Shakespeare was not only familiar with *The History of the Kings of Britain*, the magical history set out by Geoffrey of Monmouth, but also with the prophecies of Thomas the Rhymer. In a certain play, which it is traditionally unlucky to name, a clear adaptation of one of Thomas's verses is found. The original reads:

> Feddarate Castle sall ne'er be ta'en
> Till Fyvie wood to the seige is gaen.

Although these lines were adapted by Shakespeare to the castle of High Dunsinane, they were not proven true until a later century, when the troops of William of Orange made battering rams out of Fyvie wood, and entered the previously unconquered castle of Fedderate.

Like Merlin, or Nostradamus, or the Brahan Seer, Thomas has left a series of predictions as partial proof of the effectiveness of his initiation. As with many prophecies some are incomprehensible, others have been found accurate, but puerile demands of accuracy or vindication of the Otherworld powers overlook the essential importance of such individuals as Thomas.

THOMAS THE RHYMER

Whereas many of the magical ballads consist of action, or action combined with visionary sequences, the traditional variants of Thomas the Rhymer are constructed from a series of interrelated visions, which are part of one united vision and initiation sequence. As this is one of the major keys to the Underworld journey, it is worthy of careful examination and explanation, and will repay continued meditation and application. A long and complex Romance text exists, in which many of the specific elements of Garden, Fruit, Otherworld and related symbols are amplified in a conventional manner, but we will deal only with variants found in an oral tradition.

The plot moves through seven specific stages:

1. the Vision of the Queen of Elfland;
2. the Journey through the Underworld;
3. the Vision of the Tree;
4. the Ritual of Bread and Wine;
5. the Vision of the Three Roads;

6. the Vow of Silence;
7. the Return to the Upper Earth.

In some variants the order of the stages is different, while others give
descriptions of Elfland and connected material; but the sequence given
above, taken from the traditional source ballad used as our main example (pp. 55–6), is the correct magical order of events.

The Vision of the Queen of Elfland (verses 1–5)

The seer or dreamer lies upon a grassy bank, beneath a hawthorn tree.
The hawthorn tree, growing upon a grassy bank, is the Tree of Initiation
or of Commencement.

This is the tree which early legends described as being composed of
living green leaves and of flames, divided vertically, as in the vision of
the knight Peredur.

The thorn tree is one of the triad of oak, ash, and thorn, the three
sacred trees of oral tradition, to which other trees may be added from
ancient lore. This triad, however, is of considerable importance in
connection to the Three Underworld Trees. Thorn is the tree at the Gate
between the Worlds, with its associations with May ceremonies, ill luck
if picked at the wrong time, combined beauty of blossom and pain of
thorn. Hawthorn, incidentally, is also a fruit-bearing tree, and at one
time the fruit was eaten and preserved. Like the rose, it carries blossom,
thorns and fruit, showing in nature the three stages of transformation:
promise, pain and fulfilment. In the ballad of Tam Lin, Fair Janet
summons Tam from faeryland by pulling roses and breaking thorns. We
may regard the hawthorn and the rose as symbolically identical, and
may further equate them with the Crown of Thorns of the Crucifixion.

Oak is the tree of the Guardian, and of the Sacrificed Ones. In
traditional magical visions, the way to the Underworld or to the Grail
Castle is often marked by a small oaken door with a symbol carved
above it. In some versions of the Vision, the Orchard of Paradise, or the
Apple Tree Upon the Hill, is surrounded by a ring of oaks. Those who
meet the male Guardian may encounter him at an oak tree, while those
who are blessed like Thomas of Ercledoune are guided by the Queen of
Elfland direct to the fruit.

Ash, traditionally used for thrones, spears and sea-going vessels, may
be equated with the third Underworld tree, that of mediation.

The entire subject of detailed tree symbolism represents a very wide
and complex field, which is not directly relevant to the present study,

but the serious student or enquirer should consider native tree lore in depth.

A detailed study of ancient or oral tree lore is not a prerequisite of operational magic, and once again we should stress that basic initiatory patterns from common consciousness are far more important than scholarly or poetical attributions of woodland.

Thomas of Ercledoune, meanwhile, sleeps under the hawthorn tree. He beholds a 'lady gay' riding towards him. She is dressed in green, riding upon a horse, and her bridle is hung with silver bells. She is a nature power, the Isis of the ancients. Thomas erroneously titles her as 'mighty Queen of Heaven', and she immediately corrects him.

This apparently trivial detail of flattery is a very significant magical clue, which reveals important laws and powers of operation. Firstly, the human magician or initiate, whether male or female, is apt to confuse innerworld powers readily. Most modern occultists are so shocked at actually contacting any being whatsoever that they invariably confuse the communication out of sheer surprise at their own partial success. The ballad teaches us two important rules or laws: (1) Do not confuse the powers one with another; (2) The powers themselves will tell you who or what they are.

In the case of rule (1) a power or being will only react properly if properly addressed, if you know the Name, and an incorrect understanding of an innerworld being leads to flawed responses and energies *within the initiate*. There is no question of beings 'compelled' to be 'beneficial' by use of their names; this is juvenile and ignorant drivel. The beings are true to their own nature, but our understanding and channelling of that nature operates utterly through our own consciousness and physical bodies.

If we apply a power wrongly (call it by the wrong name, worship it as God, use it for foolish ends), then a self-perpetuating distortion occurs within our own matrix of body/consciousness. The Queen that approaches Thomas is the Queen of Elfland, and she specifically tells him that she is not the Queen of Heaven.

She is in fact, an Underworld or under-earth power, who manifests in upper nature as growth, shown by her green skirt; sexual power of the body, shown by the horse; and the act of summoning or banishing, shown by the silver bells. These bells, which we may equate with the ancient sistrum of the Mysteries, feature frequently in traditional lore, and are associated with motion, the wind, speed and arousal.

Rule (2) is initially common sense, for Otherworld beings are self-declared by their symbolic appearance. A tradition, however, will also give specific clues and rules, via the instructional tales, songs and dramas preserved in common consciousness. It is vitally important to avoid the pitfalls represented by the models of psychology and 'unified' symbology, wherein all aspects of dream or vision are stuffed into intellectually contrived moulds for preservation and future labelling. All symbolism is *not* related to each and every part of the psyche and the universe, and both the psychological-materialist model and the religious-unity model that are rife in our modern culture are capable of great damage through their vapid lack of direction.

It is correct to state that the various symbolic entities merge one into the other, but this occurs only through transformation within the apprehending consciousness. In other words, we have to change before the links between the various keys and gates become active. In magical work, each innerworld being should be dealt with according to its own true appearance and nature, and the powers of one realm or world should not be forced through the matrices of another. As we shall soon discover, the Queen of Elfland may become the Queen of Heaven, but she is not so to our limited perceptions.

Thomas is obliged to go with the Queen – he has summoned her up from below, and has learnt her true name and nature. In some versions of the story, they embrace beneath the tree. The seer has aroused the inner power, and it carries him away. That this power is explicitly linked with sexual arousal is no mere coincidence, but an applied use of the inner life energies for specific ends.

Thomas is bound to the Queen for seven years (a period that appears in the ballads frequently in connection with vows, and applies to the old custom of 'trial' marriages derived from pre-Christian cultural patterns based upon inner or magical laws). We find this pattern repeated in the ballad of Lord Bateman, which represents a similar pattern of operation.

Thomas mounts upon the milk white steed, and they ride off together, 'and aye whene'er the bridle rang/The steed flew swifter than the wind.'

This concludes the first stage of the visionary sequence, and leads into:

The Journey through the Underworld (verses 6–8)

The magical steed is directed into the Underworld, where neither Sun nor Moon are seen. The aroused power is directed downwards, and the imaginative ability of the seer or initiate perceives (a) a river of blood, and (b) a roaring sea. He is not, remember, wandering loosely in this potent realm, but is under the guidance of the Queen of Elfland, with whom he has exchanged vows.

We shall find the river of blood and the roaring sea again in another context, but they represent the individual's own bloodstream and flow of consciousness, perceived and experienced for the first time as identical with the greater blood and waters of created nature.

Any reasonably competent meditator will be able to confirm the *sound* of the roaring sea for him or herself, as this is a definite and commonly experienced inner sound that arises during certain stages of meditation. Deeper aspects of the sea and the blood are reached through the Underworld journey, and are not usually accessible by regular or popularized meditational methods.

This experience or mode lasts forty days and nights for Thomas, and they emerge on the other side and ride further, until they come to 'a garden tree'.

The Vision of the Tree (verses 8–9)

Thomas and the Queen of Elfland now arrive at the second tree. They have passed beneath, waded the river of blood, heard the roaring of the sea, and then have ridden *further on* to the Apple or Fruit Tree that stands in the centre of the Underworld. It is the Tree of Transformation as Thomas is soon to discover.

The fruit is usually the apple, or in some versions it is a tree of mixed fruits, as in the ancient Irish legends. We now come to the true order of the giving and taking of fruits, which is well known to be corrupted in the orthodox Christian variants of the Garden myth.

Thomas sees the fruit in its pure or unadapted state, as it grows at the heart of the Underworld. He is comprehending the energies and the powers that hold creation together, and has travelled directly to this stage upon the magical horse, guided by his partner the Queen of Elfland. As he has not met the Guardian, or been imprisoned, or exchanged riddles, or done battle, we may assume that this visionary sequence is the guiding pattern for the individual who has already undergone these processes.

If for example, Thomas were to pluck the fruit and try to eat it, the Guardian would be summoned. But he understands the true nature of his adventure, and offers to pluck the fruit as a gift to the Queen of Elfland. It is this act of simple sacrifice and direction that enables Thomas to continue his journey unchallenged, and furthermore, it is his offering of the fruit that transforms both himself *and the Queen*.

The Ritual of Bread and Wine (verses 10–11)

She advises him not to touch the fruit, for it holds all the plagues of hell. In its raw state, the fruit is poison. This advice is similar or parallel to an earlier admonition (omitted in our present text) that the river of blood is made of all the blood shed in the human world.

The Queen has a loaf of bread and a bottle of red wine, however, which she offers to Thomas. This is her response, her return of offered gifts, and they are the fruit transformed. In the Christian mass, as in the pagan, the bread is the Body, and wine the Blood. Both are transformed from the primal fruit.

If Thomas had eaten of the raw fruit, he would have been poisoned, and it is for this reason that the Guardian is placed at the approach to the tree. Once past the Guardian, the fruit has to be offered to the Queen, who now may transform the fruit into bread and wine, and herself into a deeper manifestation of Divine power.

It is incorrect to assume that this symbolic sequence shows a crude 'Christianizing' of a pagan Paradise myth. The sequence is exact and precise, and the difference between the pagan and Christian aspects of the Mystery are intimately linked to the Harrowing of Hell by Christ, which enables the human initiate to pass to and fro in His Name.

Once Thomas has partaken of the transformed fruit, given to him by the Queen, he has actually *replaced* the fruit upon the tree – by consuming it, by absorbing it into his own entity. This is such a significant action that it demands further attention.

Thomas may not pluck the fruit, for it absorbs all the plagues of hell, or all the sorrows of man and woman (in some versions). He offers to pluck it for the Queen of Elfland, and she responds by offering him bread and wine. If we filled out this section of the vision in detail, we might see that (a) Thomas does not actually pluck the fruit; he is willing to make that sacrifice without any conditions, but he is not required to do so. The implication is that this magical action is a lesser part, on the behalf of any individual, of some greater or spiritual sacrifice.

Thomas may reach the Tree of Transformation, but when he does so, the poisoned fruit is a deeper aspect of his own aroused fire, the power that has brought him through the Underworld. He sees it as part of and in union with the normally modified powers of creation that are expressed in *form* in the outer or upper world. He is now confronted with *force*, the powers behind the form, and must therefore attune or offer these to their correct place and mode of operation. This is the Queen of Elfland.

We could say that at this stage (b) the fruit disappears from the Tree, as a result of his offer of selflessness. It appears in the lap of the Queen, as bread and red wine, which she offers to him, with the suggestion that he may rest at this stage of the journey. The greater journey has not finished yet, but the traveller may rest and partake of the elements of the ritual of transformation beneath the tree.

When Thomas eats and drinks, he *re-transforms* the elements by their absorption within his entity. This is stage (c) of the central process, for at this stage, the fruit reappears upon the Tree. Thomas has effectively changed the fruit, for it *reappears in a different place upon the tree.*

The entire sequence is one of polarity and catalysation, and must be considered carefully and meditatively to reveal its fullest insights.

The Vision of the Three Roads (verses 11–14)

Once Thomas has taken the elements of bread and wine, he rests with his head upon the knee or lap of the Queen of Elfland. He is joined to her in trust, and this parallels the sexual implication of their vows and embraces in earlier verses and variants, although by this stage the concept of physical gratification has been transformed into an exchange of gifts and a shared journey and vision.

She shows him 'wonders three', a vision within a vision, and the last stage of the journey. He would not be able to perceive this stage, let alone undertake to travel upon it, if he had not undergone the rituals of transformation at the second tree.

Once again, we should emphasize that the vision of the three roads is ancient and potent, and is not to be regarded as a mere orthodox gloss upon a pagan original. Even at this last stage of the journey, the initiate is offered a choice of how he or she may use the transformed power. The three choices are:

1.   The Broad Road of wickedness that some say leads to heaven;
2.   the Narrow Road of righteousness, beset with thorns and briars;
3.   the Bonny or Middle Road, to Elfland.

The first road is that of power expressed within the outer world, that of dominion, and the illusion of worldly hierarchies that impose order in the name of heaven. It represents not only the individual propensity for simple 'wickedness' but more esoterically the law that causes materially expressed hierarchies of spiritual or magical power to degenerate and become corrupt.

The adept is able to walk this road, either for personal ends or for time-bound hierarchical schemes of order and mass control. In either case they may seem to be the road to Heaven, but terminate in evil.

The second road is that of individual sacrifice for specific aims. It represents the magical sacrifices of the ancient sacred kings, and the Sacrifice of Christ, which was a similar act upon a greater scale with far-reaching implications that are still developing in outer serial time. It may indeed be 'personal righteousness', but there is no moral issue at stake, for it is the ancient sacrifical way of containment and restriction of life-power for specific ends.

This road is also available to the adept, but the implications of the Harrowing of Hell are that the third road is now open to any that are able to perceive it.

The third road, 'to fair Elfland', is the middle of the three roads. In the detailed vision, it may lead to the Secret Castle that houses the Grail, or to a low hill on which the third tree grows. This is the Tree of Mediation, the transmuted Grail, the power of the Underworld transformed through human consciousness to encompass all worlds. It is to this place, upon the third road, that Thomas and the Faery Queen 'this night maun gae'.

The Vow of Silence (verse 15)

Thomas is advised not to speak while in faeryland, no matter what wonders are shown to him. This motif occurs in the Grail legends also, where it is tied to the asking of significant questions, a process usually associated with the confrontation of the Guardian. In a deeper understanding of this admonition at the final stage of the journey, we may find some significant magical laws.

If Thomas speaks a word, he will not get back to his own country. This popular concept, which includes not only asking questions but eating of Otherworld food and consorting with Otherworld lovers, both of which Thomas has already done, masks a magical law. As we are regarding the journey as a visionary and powerful transforming sequence, we now encounter the last choice upon the way.

Thomas may speak and question the wonders that he perceives, but by doing so, he commits himself forever to the Otherworld. He becomes, in modern terminology, an inner plane adept. He chooses to explore and grow within the inner realms and not to return to the outer world. This is one of the choices offered to the initiate after physical death, and as we are considering the most recondite levels of the Mystery, we should consider this warning from the Queen of Elfland in such a light. Should Thomas direct his attentions towards further Mysteries, he will take the fourth road, which is unseen on the other side of the hill.

If he does not do so, he is able to return by the middle way to the outer world, where he appears transformed by his experience. The three roads may also be considered in the context of post-mortem metaphysics. The discarnate soul usually takes the 'broad broad way', in company with millions of others, following certain natural laws of attraction which are attuned by specific religions and mysteries, national group-souls, deep long-term aims of potent groups and patterns. These in turn are loosely related to certain stellar influences, and to the overall luminous attraction of Lucifer within the earth's planetary body. The broad way leads to rebirth.

The road of thorns and briars represents a voluntary incarnation in service of some higher aim or order — one who need not return to the planet or group worlds by impulse or attraction, but who chooses to do so out of love for those who suffer.

The middle way does not lead to incarnation from the inner to outer worlds, under normal circumstances. It may be specifically opened for communication and exchange 'across time', and this is the simplest human level of its so-called discarnate operation. If the reader has followed the theory of the Underworld initiation carefully, it will be clear that the usual concepts of life/death are irrelevant in such a context.

In a second level or mode, the middle way is available for exchange of energies between beings in different worlds. Spiritual enlightenment flows along this way, as do many of the concerted group rituals that involve beings of more than one realm or world operating together.

The third and most significant level of the middle way is the approach of the Saviour or Messiah. It is along this way that a Divine One is born into the outer world, hence the conceptual structure of the Virgin Birth. This process, however, is merely a human reflection by Divine Power of the Descent into Hell, which is also a death/birth on the part of the Son of Light. The Descent into Hell is synonymous and simultaneous with the Conception, Birth, Sacrifice, Death and Resurrection. They only appear to be separated to the awareness locked into the illusion of serial time.

The Return to Upper Earth (verse 16)

These are the choices, then, that Thomas has taken. He has emulated Christ in his descent into hell, but has no personal motive therein. He chooses not to pass on to the unknown, but to return to the human group-world, where he acts as a prophet and as an example to all who may follow.

He is clothed in green, which signifies his union with the land, a union that occurred as a direct result of his transformation within the Underworld. His prophetic ability arises as a result of his mediating power, and not through the communication of 'familiar spirits'. He is able to perceive the apparent future, because it has already happened in the Underworld.

The importance of Thomas, and of other historical persons who undertook the journey, is not merely poetical or inspirational. They still exist, they may still be contacted, and they are present in the inner worlds as teachers and guides.

Appendix 5 The Original Underworld Visualization

(from *The Underworld Initiation*)

The following visualization is the first Underworld narrative that I developed in the 1970s, mainly from dreams and meditative visions. As this has been used by a fairly large number of people around the world, it is worth including here as a well-tested visualization. The narrative moves through a ground-plan or map of the Elements, progressing downwards in a spiralling sequence (see Figure 8). Some working notes are given from the original commentary, after the visualization text.

THE UNDERWORLD NARRATIVE

The following pages should be used as a story, similar to the old faery tales, and read to a gathering of people, who relax and employ their imagination to build up the simple images employed in the tale. Like all faery tales, it grows more powerful with familiarity and does not wear thin, but reveals an increasing depth of symbolism and meaning arising from within the gathered group.

The notes which follow the story give some insight into the magical operation involved, and both the story and the notes should be read and re-read by the individual who intends to lead or partake in such a journey.

For those who wish to use the narrative in meditation, a recorded version with specially composed music is available from the author in cassette form, from Sulis Music, BCM 3721, London, WC1N 3XX.

The Underworld Narrative

(Music, customary opening signs, etc.)

Voice
You have decided to take a journey, an Otherworld journey. Like any journey, in any world, it will have clear and definite stages; but the Otherworld journey is easier in many ways than outerworld travelling, for you are carried onwards by your own awareness, and your own will.

If you meet with difficulties upon the way, they come from within yourself, and not from anywhere else. To return from the Otherworld journey is easy, and instantaneous. Once you have travelled an inner path, you do not need to completely retrace your steps, but merely will yourself gently back to wherever you are sitting at this moment, your moment of initiation. The Otherworld journey demands effort at visualization, but the outerworld return is achieved by a sign or signal that you know and recognize. (*The sign is given here or visualized.*)

The Otherworld which you are going to visit is known very well to you, but it is not in the past or the future, but in the living present within. This is where it always has been, and always will be, present within your own awareness. The landscape and beings of the Otherworld are real within their own dimension, and should not be treated as fantasies or illusions. If you regard them as such they will respond as such, and your experience of the Otherworld will dissolve into a meaningless dream. If you recognize the reality of the inner beings they will behave according to the laws of the world in which they live, and of which they are an integral part. It may be that you have not visited this Otherworld for a long period of outer time, and you should have a firm grasp of the simple laws that hold it together during your stay therein.

One: Be aware of your intention to keep to the way that leads to whatever you seek.

Two: Do not fear distractions, do not follow them.

Three: Respond to those who give you love, and respect those who act as guardians.

With these three simple rules, you can pursue your path in peace, to whatever you will find at its end. But first you have to find the path, which is not as far away as you might think, nor is it as difficult or dangerous as you have been led to believe! As you listen, you are sitting in a place that leads directly to the path; and now the path opens up before you, within your own awareness and nowhere else.

The first step is merely to pass from the Outerworld to the Innerworld. This is achieved by relaxing, and breathing carefully in rhythm, with your eyes closed. (*Here a musical sequence, or other known signal or pulse for passing within is given.*)

Gradually you become aware of tiny points of light upon a dark blackness. They are the stars in a night sky, and they are above you as you look at them. You are lying upon the ground, looking directly up at the stars. The sky is clear, and the stars are suddenly bright and cold. The earth beneath you is hard, and it is winter. You stand up and see that you are between two huge upright stones. You look ahead, and see a faint path across the plain, lit only by starlight.

You take a few steps forward, and a crescent moon rides in the sky ahead You walk briskly down the path, and the air is cold, clean, fresh and exciting. You breathe deeply, and feel fit and full of power. The path seems familiar and yet intriguing, and you feel that it leads to a secret and special place.

Across the plain you walk, and gradually your path slopes down between shadowy hills, down and down into a valley with a stream running through it. The way ahead is guarded by two huge hills, one on each side of the valley. For a moment you look up at them, and fires flicker from their tops. You realize that the way is watched, and that you have been allowed to pass through in safety.

Now the ground levels out, and ahead of you a mist is rising. The path leads straight into the mist, and above it you can see the moon, now growing full, a white disc above the strange swirling clouds that flood across the pathway. You pause, and then step into the mist.

For a moment you lose your sense of direction, but the path feels clear beneath your feet, and you follow it carefully. As your eyes adjust to the misty light you see that the way is built of countless numbers of stones, worn smooth, as if by the passage of many feet through thousands of years. Each stone shines gently with a very slight pale light, like the reflection of a full moon.

The ground around you is growing soft and marshy, and you catch glimpses of long reedy grass and pools of water through the mist. The air is growing damper and somehow warmer, as you follow the ancient stones of the pathway. Around you are the muffled sounds of the marsh; it is alive with the secret life of under-roots and beneath-stones. There are creatures that crawl and slide and hop, there are splashes and faint cries of fear and alarm from the water.

Nothing touches the path. The path leads on into the swirling mists which thicken and thicken until you see nothing, hear nothing, and only feel the ground beneath your feet.

You stop. You look, but see only a white mass of warm swirling vapour. You feel a closeness, a presence upon the path ahead, but you do not know what it is. Do you dare to walk forward? You will yourself to take another step . . . you want to shout out, 'Who's there? Who are you?', but you keep silent.

A tiny cold wind blows along the path from behind you, parting the thick mist suddenly. You see a huge lump of shadow, a towering black shape with massive spreading horns, and it bars the way utterly. The mist parts fully now, and the light of a bright full moon streams down upon the way. You see that the beast before you is a cow ... a white cow with long curved horns. She looks directly at you, and after a moment, begins to turn away. As she turns, you see that she has a curious mark upon her shoulder. She begins to walk ahead of you now, guiding you along the path. You follow her confidently, she knows the way, and the mists return to swirl and blow across the swamp.

Now you come to a branching of the way, where it parts into three. The path to the right opens out suddenly into a broad paved roadway that curves easily into the distant mists. It looks inviting and interesting, and was obviously built for some special purpose. The path to the left curves steeply off behind you, back up to the watching hills. It is piled with loose stones, and you see it climb up and up out of sight. It seems that either path will take you out of the marsh, and out of the constant mists; but the way ahead, the continuation of the path on which you stand, leads straight on into the steaming clouds of vapour.

At this junction of the ways is a little rise of ground, and on it grow a few small trees and bushes, dominated by a tall deeply carved standing stone.

Look closely at the image which guards the parting of the ways.

The warm mists swirl about it as soon as you have seen it, and so you turn to consider the right hand way. The broadly paved stones are littered with objects, with metal rings and bracelets, carved gems and precious ancient workmanship.

Now you consider the left hand way, and just beyond the junction there is a little mound of stones with a skull set into a niche within. This skull looks up the pathway, and seems to warn against coming back down.

Which path is best? Which way should you turn? All three seem to carry both opportunity and danger. Suddenly, the cow stamps her hoof, and sets off down the middle way into the mist. In an instant you realize that for you there is no question of hesitation, no doubt as to the way ahead. You follow her into the unknown.

All around you now is water, with steam swirling from it. You hear a curious bubbling sound, and tall rough rocks appear on either side of the path which weaves a serpent way between them. The water rises, and the steam is heady and hot, with a curious smell of earth and minerals. The path coils round and round in a tight spiral, heading always to the right between the rocks.

Suddenly you realize that the white cow has disappeared! The path stops before a huge tumble of natural rocks, out of which pour streams of hot water, and the rocks are shining with a wet red colour like blood.

Growing up out of the rock is an enormous tree, that reaches far far up into the steamy air. A curious glow seems to emerge from the stones, and you can see by this earthlight that the tree has an enormous crown of rustling branches and leaves. As the wind blows, you can hear many birds and animals moving and calling within the branches.

The path has stopped, the guide is gone
from here you travel on alone.
Look closely in between the stones,
and you will see a pathway leading down.
Down into the mother earth
whose deep womb gives the waters birth,
down into the steam and dark,
where no light gives you way or mark —
down and down and down you crawl
into the deepest deepest hall.
Down beyond all sense or rhyme,
down beyond all thought or time,
down and down and down you go,
until you hear a sound below:
a sound mysterious and deep
that throbs and wakes your blood from sleep —
the sound that brings the waters forth
out of the living heart of earth:
a sound of whirling rushing air,
a sound of blazing burning fire,
and from your narrow single way
you see a glow like coming day,
and as with every dark-filled night —
you leap out at the end . . .
to light!

(Narrative pauses here. Suitable music, or silent pause. At the end of this period, the agreed signal for returning is given.)

'Awake now! Awake! For you have been blessed by the power that moves your life within you. Awake, and return peacefully to your Outerworld.

The way is short and clear,
open your eyes, and you are sitting . . .
here!

Depart in peace, and remember all that you have seen and heard and felt. Take it with you to transform the outer world; let it pass from you as power into all that is alive . . . that the land may be blessed, and the growing plants, and the creatures of the land, and the men and women and children in your care.

For we are priests and priestesses of power
until the end of time

In the name of . . . .

(Closing music if required. A period of readjustment. Then notes should be made immediately, or if a group, there should be discussion with notes taken. Each individual should also write up their experiences later; as material is often triggered by later circumstances, or memories.)

Operative Notes for Narrative

The structure of the narrative is fourfold:

1. Instructional commencement;
2. magical action (the journey);
3. contemplative/mystical (inner reaction);
4. outer dedication – giving out to the land the energies released.

These four stages correspond to the four quarters of the magical circle. They are not necessarily of the same duration in serial time, and may be varied objectively or subjectively according to circumstances or requirements.

Operation of the magical processes

Despite the assurance regarding the ease and safety of passing between the worlds (a perfectly valid assurance for the beginner operating alone or in a group, where limited action is usually safeguarded by inner or outer mediators of the early stages of the Mystery), the action calls for a deliberate opening of the way by an experienced operator, during the 'breathing' and 'opening' references in the text. The narrative may be read or recorded with suitable music for playback.

Note that the would-be initiate is not helped through this opening, and certainly not *put* through it. The experienced mediator merely energizes the opening of the pillars that leads to the innerworld about to be described. The new traveller is free to choose how he or she will respond, according to personal abilities and limitations.

The narrative is keyed to a specific physical location, as well as the innerworld described, so it is essential for at least one participant to have passed within at the physical locus. Without this experience of attuning, the journey will not be fully keyed to the innerworld required. Most symbolic or Otherworld journeys are actually keyed to physical places or sites, and for this work, a human must have made the journey at the actual site concerned. But there is no necessity for it to be always made there, or that each passing within must be done at the actual locus.

Ideally, the most powerful situation would be a group of experienced mediators who regularly pass within upon the site of the physical manifestation of the Otherworld concerned. The physical body becomes attuned to the site by this process, and the power available is considerably amplified.

An experienced mediator should be present to visualize and energize all stages of the journey, with the basic rule that the new traveller is always free to choose at the various stages. The guiding action of the mediator stops, however, when the initiate enters the passage down into the earth, regardless of previous experience, with the words 'The Path has stopped, the guide has gone, from here you travel on alone.'

From this point each individual travels alone, no matter how new or old they are to the experience. The adept may then use whatever ability in invocation he or she has, during the culmination or devotion, but is generally receptive after the inner power has been contacted.

This change of mode from active to passive is very important in operations of this type, and is the key to success and harmonious working.

The totem beast, it should be added, is not symbolic of the mediator, but is an innerworld being in its own right, which works for all travellers equally.

The closing section of the narrative should be a very deliberate emerging and closing down, carried out as effectively as possible by the adept.

Notes on the Journey

The first emerging between the pillars leads to a night and winter landscape, with a deliberate radical alteration of situation and position. The traveller has moved from indoors to outdoors, sitting in comfort to lying on hard ground, warmth to cold, known to unknown, etc.

This is not an easy transition to visualize, for a beginner, but with a properly energized opening-of-the-way, it should make an effective transfer providing there is some suspension of disbelief on the part of the initiate. It is also intended as a means of getting travellers moving as quickly as possible, not allowing opportunities to drift or sit about examining the inner landscape.

Note that although the script moves in four stages around the circle, ESWN, the inner action reverses this direction (i.e. Instructional East, Magical South, Mystical West, Active giving North, as described above).

Inwardly, the journey starts at the North, in Winter. From the plain beneath the stars, the traveller moves from Earth to Water (travelling N–W), and then moves inwards and downwards, towards the centre of the metaphysical cycle, reaching where the Elements originate in the heart of all Being. From here, the traveller emerges to the dawning light of the East, and should move to the South, or maximum Light. In culmination, the circle is continued to the West as reception or contemplation, around to the North as fulfilment and completion by giving, and so emerging again in the East to commence ordinary outer life afresh.

1.   Commence initial 'Journey'. Introduction;
2.   Emerge North, pass to West;
3.   Path to Waters and Tree of Life;
4.   Down tunnel to Underworld, out to East;
5.   Increasing light to South;
6.   Contemplation to West;
7.   Return to North for action of giving out;
8.   Begin again in Outerworld.
(see Figure 8)

This order of motion is a circular expression of the Secret Way across the Abyss, suggested in the Qabalah. This mode of consciousness is extremely important in the Western Mysteries, particularly the specific Otherworld Mysteries of Britain.

The 'secret way' actually passes *through* the Abyss, but by a known and operable path, rather than in chaos. It was this path, for example, that the Gnostics believed was used by Christ to incarnate secretly, by passing the orders of angels via a power pattern that would not be visible to the innerworlds until his return.

The way is called 'The Path of the Thief'. The Roman Christian variant of this 'secret' was worked into the myth of the Harrowing of Hell, which is a restatement of the quest of Arthur to the Otherworld, where he and his band of heroes descend below to gain gifts for their people. This is the origin of the later medieval allegories of the Holy Grail, a sophistication of the cauldron of the Otherworld that was gained by the Welsh Arthur.

The principle is found in all metaphysics, and is especially important for the practice of effective magic. Whereas the Elements and related powers have a specific cycle (symbolized by the Four Directions around the Circle and epitomized in nature by the Four Seasons, etc.), humankind is able to work this same 'secret path' as was taken by the Son of

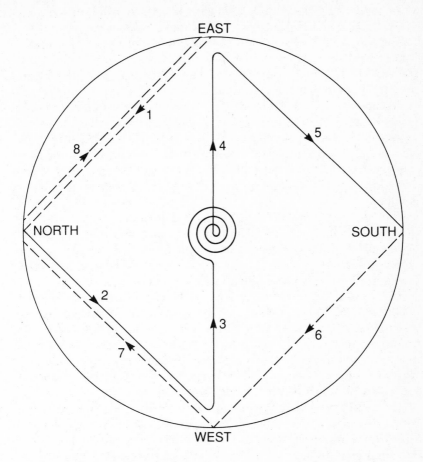

Figure 8 The Descent into the Underworld mapped through
the Elements and Directions.

Light (under whatever name), either through the power of spiritual
meditation, or through the inherent divinity in mankind.

More accurately stated, and less susceptible to propaganda and
corruption, the path is a fact of metaphysics, which is open to all and any
able to assemble the component energies and put them into action.
Despite this fact, most individuals work this way under the blessing or
protection of some symbolic great being, and the path commences in
the North under the power of Auriel (for the magician who works
Qabalah), or of the Sisters at the Back of the North Wind who mediate
the death power of the Goddess; and in either case the commencement

is via the gift of grace, or reflected light and wisdom from the stars, in a manner gentle enough to be received without imbalance.

The travelling N–W is the breaking-down, the return to primeval water as the mist grows thicker in the narrative imagery. The path is well indicated, and has been well travelled. Those that have gone before have left light in every stone for us to follow.

Perhaps the earliest travellers would have had to struggle their way through the elemental earth/water dissolution, hence their praise as heroes in the folk sagas and tales, but the continued effort of those who have gone before has made the way clear and safe, providing the rules suggested are followed carefully. There is always danger, the greatest being that of distraction, which for some people can occupy many lifetimes.

The watchers from the hilltops are symbolically in the Northern Quarter. They are *voluntary* Guardians of various sorts, both human and non-human. This was achieved in ancient time by a specific sacrifice whose reflection/phantom was set to watch the sacred site, to protect the people, and to communicate through chosen priestesses.

These guardians were tied to the area 'between the worlds' for a set period of outer time, established by actual solar rotation (passage of planet around Sun), after which they were released and replaced. On release, these individuals made their way via the Middle Path to the innerworlds of their Mystery, or returned around the great outside path to reincarnation. This is only the briefest summary of this important matter, which is dealt with at length elsewhere.

The Left Hand Path, therefore, as defined within the narrative, has a ban upon it, for the individual may travel up it at will (as a voluntary Guardian) but not back down, as he/she is then subject to certain laws of limitation of energy, and must work through the power-pattern of the Guardian process. This definition covers various aspects of the Left Hand Path upon the Tree of Life, and will differ in intensity and in expression according to each individual. The greatly abused concepts of self-sacrifice, death, the devil, etc., are intimately connected with understanding and experience of this Path or group of Paths.

The Right Hand Path referred to traverses the circle WSEN, and is the way of working out in the outer world, through major outer action, effective history, etc. Strong individual cases upon this path may be leaders, dictators and the like, but more simply it represents a return to the outer group-world, with no desire to pursue the inner journey further. From an esoteric point of view, it is the Path of Distraction if misunderstood and misapplied.

The totem beast, the White Cow, has appeared during the dissolving phase of the work (refer also to alchemical symbols) and is a key image of the ancient lunar power. She is strength, fertility, motherhood, and her horns are the great horns of Power.

This guide is *not* the operating human adept, but a potent inner power focus. The mark upon her shoulder is extremely important, and is likely to vary for individuals, if it is present. This mark is usually the identifying symbol of the innerworld order to which the human initiate has affinities, or which is involved in the current magical operation. The totem beast is by no means limited to a mere fertility totem, and the place of the cow and the midwife Brigid in Celtic lore is vitally important to an understanding of the Western Mysteries. It is the cow that brings you back to birthpoint after your dissolution.

The image cut into the stone that marks the crossroads works in a similar manner, but represents a 'higher octave' or deeper level of mediation. Whereas the totem beast carries the code of an innerworld order, the marking stone carries the symbol of a great being, or 'god'.

One might expect the image to be that of the Son of Light, but others also occur. Strictly speaking the image is likely to be that of the Hung God, the sacrificed Sun rather than the triumphant Sun, a key which pre-dates Christian use.

The 'secret' image here is that of a dark figure in tattered cloak, who is impaled or hung with arms outstretched. He has four faces, one for each road.

The entire journey occurs during the phases of the Moon, from dark to full. This is not a journey of 'rising in the planes' as is commonly done in modern magic or meditation, but the way to light through darkness. It goes Underground at the point at which normal pathworking would move round into the Sun. By so doing, it traverses the secret way to the Mother, which activates the Light Son/Daughter energies within each individual.

The complete vision involves a realization of the unity of the male/female powers with and without as One (the so-called Son of Light is actually bisexual). The mediation phase of the narrative, however, is left unguided, to develop according to the needs of each individual. The last stage of the journey is made alone, and the Presence is met in silence.

Prior to this stage, however, the guide (cow) disappears without the traveller being aware of her passing. In other words, once the initiate has reached this point in the journey, the guiding power is no longer needed. At this stage the dissolving power has reached the centre of the elemental circle, and some real awareness should be achieved of both the Elemental Powers and of the Tree of Life, as living forces and not mere intellectual definitions.

It is this awareness that causes the opening between the stones to occur, and the initiate crawls down this alone. For the trained adept, who is able to operate the specific tuning required for 'the Path of the Thief', this is a magical pattern which becomes established and potentially unlimited with continued application and development.

For the less experienced traveller, the phasing and direction of the narrative up to this stage creates a field of consciousness which enables him/her to achieve the Entrance for the first time (in their current lifetime).

There may be more difficulty in subsequent experiences of the journey, wherein this first initiation has to be reinforced with training and magical exercises.

There is a clear and intended parallel at this stage with the ancient ritual initiations involving rock passages, using womb and tomb symbolism to trigger off awareness from earth-birth to human-birth, and finally to inner-birth in full awareness. This use of analogous keys will open awareness into regions normally inaccessible to the everyday conditioned modes of reception.

The chanting suggested during the journey into the deep is the 'word' of female/male union. In this case, the word used is likely to be that of the Mother Filled with Light, and the initiate should be familiar with this Word of Power in advance, although this is not essential for the operation to be successful (AMA AIMA AMEN).

At the emergence into light, the individual is left free to respond as best as possible to the power. Music may be used here, but a period of silence is essential. The journey down through the earth has not had any intentional terrors worked into it, but they may be present in the awareness of the traveller.

For a male, the terrors may be in the form of the Dark Mother of Death, whereas for a female it may be the image of the restrictive God. This image is the Horned God of the ancients that the Christians turned into the devil. He is both hunter and controller of beasts, and in the Tarot symbolism is a potent Guardian upon the Left Hand Path (the God of Guardians all) but not in any way 'evil'.

The way to pass beings of this sort is to ask them, without fear, what secret they guard.

The answer will change with changed awareness or circumstances, as the secret may be a knot within one's own consciousness, or a more potent magical secret altogether. Sometimes the two are tied together. Without beings of this sort, limited awareness (which is the expression of entity) would become unlimited, resulting in wild unbalance.

This is why both god and goddess of this sort are hunters, for the

Wild Hunt collects the phantoms of the recently dead. These beings are expressions of the powers of essential limitation, and hold the secrets of the central or solar consciousness of restriction. They arise as energy constructs transfer from one state or rate to another. These little-understood metaphysical laws have direct crude analogies in materialist physics.

Another way of stating this set of laws is the concept that whatever limits in one direction liberates in another. To activate such keys beneficially, they must be mediated as powers of liberation. The direction of energy flow must be from an unrequired state to a required state, and obvious reversals, errors and limitations upon imbalanced demands result in misunderstanding of the nature of 'liberty', the 'devil', 'freedom from restriction' and similar subtle matters.

In the operation of magic in particular, many initiates are deterred by their first experience of a flow of power greater than that recognized in normal life, which appears to be in conflict with cherished notions of selfhood, personality, role in life, etc. One of the great problems of magic is not 'getting it to work', but balancing its operation in a manner that will not arouse hostility and fear, both within oneself and in others. Hence the strict 'moral' conditioning required for magical work.

After passing any personal Guardians of the Heart, the Presence is encountered. An experienced mediator may invoke or link in whatever manner possible at this point in the journey; and if the path has been travelled well, the Power is present, and no further effort is needed in this final stage, which can be totally receptive.

Narratives of this type are particularly useful in dissolving disbelief and making initial magical experiences for beginners, but there is no theoretical limit to their effectiveness, and they are not mere 'infant's class' material by any means.

During the silent pause, experiences will vary considerably. They are likely to range from states of consciousness in contact with the Mother Goddess, through to key symbols for future use and development, visions, and many other types of realization.

Examples of the types of symbolism encountered include:

1. A vast underground cavern, lit by glowing sourceless light;
2. a cave with an ill-defined (or well-defined) Mother Goddess image within the rock at one end;
3. a garden in open sunlight at the centre of the earth, in which grows an apple tree;
4. a massive cyclopean temple, with a huge altar at one end;
5. an image of stars shining at the bottom of a pool or well.

All of the above are brief examples from actual workings of the narrative, but none convey the sense of Presence. Such images are merely feedback to the brain, generating acceptable images therein. These images may be true representations of the past or future, or actual experiences of constructed inner worlds.

In some cases other beings are felt to be present, generally unseen, though sometimes clearly presented. During one working, the travellers (male and female were present) saw an image of a well pool with two serpents around it. In this pool shone the stars. This is similar to the key vision of Merlin and the Dragons. As the working which gave rise to this vision was carried through on the site of an ancient spring focus, it linked with Celtic and pre-Celtic magical workings of prolonged periods.

The imagery of the well, which gives vision through the Earth to beyond time and space into the greater universe, is not limited to the Celtic cultural stream, but such a vision is of great importance in the understanding or relationship between inner and outer powers.

The mere details of the vision are only a tiny part of its overall impact in terms of consciousness within the traveller, and intellectual assimilation of details is quite irrelevant to the actual experience itself, and therefore preparation or giving of clues to the experience is usually a waste of effort. Furthermore, one of the hallmarks of a genuine inner experience is that certain key images are shared by all involved, without prior preparation or information. For reasons of this sort, so-called 'occult secrecy' may be extremely important. The crude comparison may be made between someone who has read a book or seen photographs of a distant land, and who can talk in detail about the reflections that they have intellectually assimilated, and the experience of someone who has actually been to the place itself. More significant, the traveller can bring back gifts from the distant land, whereas the reader of travel books cannot.

The return journey is made rapidly and comfortably, without a retracing of steps. This is not as shocking a concept as one might imagine, and is rooted in the magical adage that the outermost world (the Kingdom of the Qabalist) is identical to the innermost (the Crown) after another manner or mode of awareness and level of being. If the traveller can achieve some realization of the Presence, the return journey has been made automatically at its conclusion. If necessary, a period of adjusting music an be added after the closing ritual phrases.

It should be noted that the closing phrases are extracts from an actual ritual, and that the initiate returns to the outer world to mediate the

matter   Candelmar

bowl
rattle, whistle

white

<u>North</u>   midnight
          winter
          Body
          Earth
          Melancholic

stone of destiny
calling in 4 d - aligning
energy body w/ axis
in the <u>earth</u>
adamantine - steadfast
                      less

divine power, and not simply to retrace his steps and close it down behind him.

A clear division should be made, however, between effective realization of the inner Powers into the outerworld, and mere 'day-dreaming' or 'entrancement'. The narrative makes a clear difference between the innerworld journey and dreaming, and this difference is carried right through to the conclusion in manifestation. It is for this reason that the conclusion is finalized by keywords from an established and potent ritual pattern, which locks the energies into the material world in specific ways.

Repeated workings of the narrative and related material will reveal further extracts and insight into this particular ritual, which forms part of an ancient liturgy, centred around a rite known as *The Mask of the Bright One*.

Appendix 6 The Tomb of a King: Ancestral Contact at an Ancient Site

(from *The Underworld Initiation*)

This account is typical of Underworld contacts at certain (but not all) ancient sites. The ancestral contact speaks through the altered consciousness of the seer or meditator, who has used Underworld techniques to enter into the site.

INTRODUCTION

The King who appears in the following report is a sacred king, though not, perhaps, in the manner of modern books on paganism. Beings of this type are extremely important in the Western Tradition, and are not identical with the well-publicized inner plane adepts of modern occultism, who would, in fact, also apply to the sacred kings for their wisdom and understanding.

As with any esoteric or dynamic and unusual material, discretion is advised, and a leavening of humour. Not all ancient sites operate in the manner described, and some of them were never attuned to the system of symbolism and magic employed. The author does not encourage the reader to rush off and invite communication from the ancient ones at prehistoric sites, mainly because the time and energy involved are better spent on inner disciplines at home and at peace.

THE TOMB OF A KING, AT LES MONTS GRANTEZ, JERSEY

26 September 1978
This ancient prehistoric tomb is in an elevated and fairly isolated

position, very well preserved, and only recently excavated by archaeo-
logists (1912) who found it 'comparatively undisturbed'.

The King buried here had achieved his merge with the environment,
and was still available as an inner entity for dialogue and interchange of
communication. After an initial contact made by tuning to the site in
meditation, the King later appeared (away from the site itself, as the
contact unfolded or decoded itself) as an older man, very brown, with
curly hair and black beard, and spiral cheek tattoos. His eyes appeared
like large black stones, due to the visual effect of tattooing or colouring
around the deep eye sockets. He wore clothing made of skins, a tight
tunic and trousers tied around with sinews.

In communication he may be addressed as 'Earth-man' and 'Stone-
King', the nearest modern language equivalents to two magical names.
The first was his identity as king before physical death, the second an
after-death name of transformation. He was the leader of a tribe or
extended family of about fifty or sixty people at the time of his physical
death, although he implied an influence over a greater number, through
an obscure concept of family relationship that seemed to extend beyond
the Islands to both Britain and Brittany.

Some time was spent attempting to elaborate this relationship, which
was apparently of great importance in his culture, but which seems
obscure to the modern intellect. The basic pattern was one in which
various 'kings' could rule extended tribes and families over large distances, without ever conflicting with one another. The patterns of social
behaviour and warfare that resulted from this system were not similar to
the modern concept of 'territory' or 'conquest' in any way, but seemed
to be derived from 'loss of face' or a concept that meant *change of roots
in the family ground*.

The discarnate King was responsible for communicating 'Earth-peace'
to his people, this being an energy that resulted from his merging with
the environment, and finally emerging 'on the other side' of it as an
entity of wholeness or integration, able to link and mediate through
various stages of human and non-human evolution.

After initial contact, the old king was (and still is) present as a father
figure, exactly as he was to those who linked with him thousands of
years ago when this system of inner working was fully operational.
There were several obscure intimations, difficult to translate into a
contemporary world or universe-picture:

1.   The King is now part of the solar system (?) or Universe (?), linked
through the *stones* and the special structure of the dolmen and mound,
which become an Earth-power gate or amplifier for his awareness, a

focus by which his differing viewpoint may be translated into one which is accessible to physical humans still on the planet.

The curious and difficult point about this concept is the accompanying awareness that (to the King) the solar system is inside the structure of the stones and in the very bones of the Earth itself and is in no way external or removed from it. He is able to communicate this awareness very clearly indeed, and it seems to have been essential to his people's development. The effect of this awareness on the modern consciousness is rather disturbing, and is quite different from the generally accepted reality-patterns currently used by mankind trying to relate to existence.

2.   The purpose of the dolmen or passage grave is extremely precise and 'scientific'. A sealed chamber of massive stones, which have to be over a certain mass or size, is buried beneath a mound of earth. This causes certain natural processes to occur, directly due to the shapes and nature of the structure itself. This is usually aided by the knowledge and co-operation of the being or beings buried alive within it.

The aim is to achieve an integration with the Earth environment, moving through it to other states of awareness. (These are *in the Earth*, according to the King, or more strictly speaking, the Earth is *outside the stars*, and is the gateway to them.) The actual physical structure is womblike, and was identified as a returning to the Mother. There is strict time rotation involved in the process, and a guardian was placed to ensure that there was no disturbance during this period of gestation prior to inner rebirth.

Other people were also interred, either at the same time or at later stages of the development of the merge. The King suggested quite jovially that the process was voluntary, but implied a system of family obligation which could not be avoided, or a system which cast out those who did not merge when their time was due. This shocking occurrence was the greatest 'loss of Earth root' that anyone could visualize, and was the equivalent of vile and obscene anti-human crime. The thought of anyone *not* wanting merge was repulsive in the extreme, and the process was a sought-after privilege that was retained through certain family ties, and could be passed on through a female line of descent.

Once the inner integration process had occurred, the chamber was then used for consultation and intitiation. Entry was made through a tiny crawl passage, usually kept sealed and guarded by a restrained soul. This guardian was a deliberately tied sacrifice, a human who was bound for a specific period to remain in an interim state close to the outerworld, to defend the chamber against break-in and tampering. After a certain number of years (solar cycles) the guard was free, and was replaced or rendered unnecessary by the success of the King's merging. In a 'fully achieved' chamber only the King remained, but he could link to specific ancestors in spirit (*'Fathers in the deep that Earth is outside'*). The supplicant crawled in, and was left in the total darkness to communicate with the King.

The pattern is found clearly in modern magical practice, where the King is seated in the West, and one approaches him from the East, through the Pillars. The interesting point is that this King is fully able to relate to modern magical technique, and has various things to teach or communicate.

In a simple magical operation, designed to open up his specific contact in a completely different place, far from his Earth-site, the King calmly informed the operator of a mistake in the pattern of the ritual. When this error was corrected, the contact became much stronger.

The simple basis of this fraction of magical teaching was as follows:

In the tomb, the King is magically 'in the West', that is, at the end of the chamber, seated, and giving out the fullness of his awareness from his position in the depth of the womb. When an attempt was made to place him by image in the West of a modern magical temple, he informed the operator that this was quite wrong, and that the operator should be in the West, visualizing the King approaching at the East. When this was done, the inner imagery reverted to the King's own tomb, as if the two 'Wests' had come face to face.

Prior to tuning the energies in this manner, the link had been rather difficult and sporadic, causing the operator to be kept awake at night, to be aware of the King at unrequired moments, and giving a general sense of lack of tuning, searching and semi-blindness. Once the King's operational suggestion was adopted, the contact could be turned on or off at will, and became extremely balanced and clear.

The rule or pattern of tombs of this sort was general for all the dolmens and passage graves that are found in the Western culture, which can still be seen today. Some are empty and failed, but others retain their inner contact, and can be used.

One most interesting aspect of these curious 'generators' is that the flow is *two-way*. The inner King, locked in the Earth-that-is-outside-the-stars learns about your awareness, and transmits it back to his people, while you learn about their awareness, and bring it forward into your own self. The King occupies a middle or mediating 'point' in this process, conveying a type of awareness that makes nonsense of the normal conception of 'time' and 'space'. To the King, 'time' is only valid as the rotational phase prior to his merging with the Earth; it had no meaning in his original outer life, nor does it have any meaning in his evolved inner state.

On attempting to convey the meaning of the flow of time, the response from the King was the equivalent of *'there is no line of such a shape. There is only turning until you are inside the Earth. From the little turning to the great turning that is inside the little turning. Inside the great turning is Earth-peace.'*

References

1   *History of Rome*, Michael Grant, Weidenfeld & Nicolson, London, 1978.

2   *Robert Kirk, Walker Between Worlds* (a modern English edition of Kirk's *Secret Commonwealth of Elves, Fauns and Fairies* with detailed commentary), R. J. Stewart, Element Books, Shaftesbury, 1990.

3   *The Fairy Faith in Celtic Countries*, W. Y. Evans Wentz, Colin Smythe Ltd, Gerrards Cross, 1988 (reprinted from the original 1911 edition). This reprint has an excellent introduction by Kathleen Raine.

4   *The Underworld Initiation*, R. J. Stewart, Aquarian Press, 1985. Currently out of print: copies of this edition are available mail order direct from Sulis Music, BCM 3721, London WC1N 3XX.

5   *Psychology and the Spiritual Traditions*, ed. R. J. Stewart, Element Books, Shaftesbury, 1990. This anthology with essays by a range of international contributors, discusses some of the problems of 'New Age' spirituality, psychology, and their relationship to the perennial traditions of transformation and enlightenment.

6   See Kirk (2) above.

7   *Samuel Pepys* (3 vols.), Arthur Bryant, Wm Collins, London, 1938.

8   *Living Magical Arts*, R. J. Stewart, Blandford Press (HB), Poole, 1987, (PB) London, 1991. *Advanced Magical Arts*, R. J. Stewart, Element Books, Shaftesbury, 1989. *Hamlet's Mill*, H. von Dechend and G. de Santillana, Godine, Boston, 1977.

9   *Celtic Gods and Goddesses*, R. J. Stewart (illustrated Miranda Gray & Courtney Davis), Blandford Press, London, 1990.

10   Visualization cassettes are available from Sulis Music, BCM 3721, London WC1N 3XX.

11   *The Erotic World of Faery*, Maureen Duffy, Panther, London, 1974.

12   *Cuchulainn*, R. J. Stewart, Firebird Books, Poole, 1987. Also *Cuchulainn* (cassette), epic Irish poetry read by Van Morrison, on the Sulis Music label (address above).

13   *Where is Saint George?*, R. J. Stewart, Moonraker Press (HB), Bradford on Avon, 1977, Blandford Press (PB), London, 1989.

14   *The Prophetic Vision of Merlin* and *The Mystic Life of Merlin*, R. J. Stewart, Penguin Arkana, Harmondsworth, 1986.

15   *Cuchulainn*, R. J. Stewart, Firebird Books, Poole, 1988. Also *Celtic Gods, Celtic Goddesses*, see (9) above.

16   *Legendary Britain*, J. Matthews & R. J. Stewart, Blandford Press, London, 1989. *Creation Myth*, R. J. Stewart, Element Books, Shaftesbury, 1989.

17   A recording of *Thomas Rhymer* and *Tam Lin* sung in the traditional style for narrative ballads is on *More Magical Songs*, R. J. Stewart, Sulis Music, address above.

18   *Creation Myth*, as (16) above.

19   See Kirk (2) above.

20   *The Forgotten Mage*, Dolores Ashcroft-Nowicki, Aquarian Press, Wellingborough, 1987.

Further Reading

Aubert, O. L. *Legendes Traditionelles de la Bretagne*, Saint Brieuc Editions, 1970.

Branston, B. *Lost Gods of England*, Thames & Hudson, London, 1957.

Brennan, M. *Stars and the Stones*, Thames & Hudson, London, 1983.

Brewer's Dictionary of Phrase and Fable, Cassell, London, 1959.

Briggs, K. *Dictionary of Fairies*, Allen Lane, London, 1976.

Campbell, A. *Waifs and Strays of Celtic Tradition*, David Nutt, London, 1889.

Campbell, J. F. *Popular Tales of the West Highlands* (4 vols.), Wildwood House, London, 1984.

Carmichael, A. *Carmina Gadelica*, Oliver & Boyd, Edinburgh, 1928–71.

Child, F. J. *The English and Scottish Popular Ballads*, Dover Publications, New York, 1965.

De Jubainville, H. D'Arbois *The Irish Mythological Cycle*, O'Donoghue & Co., Dublin, 1903.

Douglas, Sir G. *Scottish Fairy and Folk Tales*, Walter Scott Ltd, London.

Graves, R. *The White Goddess*, Faber, London, 1948.

Green, M. *Gods of the Celts*, Alan Sutton, Gloucester, 1986.

Hartland, E. S. *English Fairy and other Folk Tales*, Walter Scott Ltd. London.

Hole, C. *English Folk Heroes*, Batsford, London, 1948.

Jobes, G. *The Dictionary of Mythology, Folklore and Symbols*, Scarecrow Press, New York, 1961.

Keightley, T. *The Fairy Mythology*, Wildwood House, London, 1981.

Kirk, R. *The Secret Commonwealth*, D. S. Brewer, Cambridge, 1976.

Lebor Gabala Erenn (The Book of Invasions), trans. R. A. S. MacAlister, Irish Texts Society, Dublin, 1938–56.

Mackenzie, D. A. *Scottish Folk-Lore and Folk-Life*, Blackie, Edinburgh, 1935.

Macleod, Fiona (William Sharp) *Poems and Dramas*, William Heinemann Ltd, London, 1933.

‗‗‗‗‗ *The Divine Adventure, Iona, Studies in Spiritual History*, William Heinemann Ltd, London, 1927.

Murray, M. *The Divine King in England*, Faber, London, 1954.

O'Rahilly, T. F. *Early Irish History and Mythology*, Dublin Institute of Advanced Studies, Dublin, 1946.

Oxford Book of Ballads, OUP, London, 1969.

Rees, A. & B. *Celtic Heritage*, Thames & Hudson, London, 1961.

Ross, A. *The Folklore of the Scottish Highlands*, Batsford, London, 1976. (Also other volumes by various authors in the *Folklore of . . .* series.)

Westwood, J. *Albion: A Guide to Legendary Britain*, Granada, London, 1985.

Wimberley, L. C. *Folklore in the English and Scottish Ballads*, Frederick Ungar & Co, New York, 1959.

Yeats, W. B. *Irish Fairy and Folk Tales*, Walter Scott Ltd, London.

Index